MER

MOM EGG REVIEW

Vol. 20 - 2022

Half-Shell Press
New York

MER - Mom Egg Review is an annual collection of poetry, fiction, creative prose, and art about mothers and motherhood.

www.momeggreview.com.

Front Cover Image: "Summer" by Michelle Gallagher.

MER is a member of the Community of Literary Magazines and Presses.

This publication has been made possible, in part, by a grants program of the New York State Council on the Arts, a state arts agency, and the Community of Literary Magazines and Presses. *MER* is grateful for this generous support.

MER thanks The Motherhood Foundation for support and sponsorship

Thanks to founding publishers, Joy Rose and Mamapalooza, and founding editor Alana Ruben Free.

MER can be purchased directly from the press on our website, through online retailers, at select independent bookstores, and through EBSCO.

Contact *MER* at MERliterary@gmail.com for info about discounts for quantity purchases or for classroom use.

ISBN: 978-0-9915107-8-8
(Half-Shell Press)

MER - Mom Egg Review
PO Box 9037
Bardonia, NY 10954

www.momeggreview.com
www.facebook.com/momeggreview
Twitter: @momeggreview
Contact: MERliterary@gmail.com

MER

MOM EGG REVIEW

Vol. 20 - 2022

Editor-in-Chief
Marjorie Tesser

Poetry Editors
Jennifer Martelli
Cindy Veach

EDITORS' NOTES

Marjorie Tesser

MER Editor-In-Chief

Our twentieth annual print issue is themed "Mother Figures," cultural icons representing motherhood. What is a mother figure? What have we been told or shown by them? What values do they reflect? What cultural learning do they assume? How does a mother figure deviate from one's own experiences?

In online poetry and prose folios this year, we have explored several aspects of the concept: "Mother in Objects," "Mothers and Children," "The Mother Role," "Storied Mothers," and "Other Mothers." Visit our website, momeggreview.com, to explore the folios.

These and other themes are investigated in the current print issue. Our contributors, established writers and emerging debut authors, responded with work that is resonant, original, and thoughtful, and which considers a dizzying range of mother figures: some worthy of emulation and some, cautionary tales, some selected and some foisted upon us. The writer may have chosen to stand outside the figure or to assume the persona. Many writers recognized lineage, a personal "mother figure," who, by existence or example, has nourished them.

Here are mothers from the classics, mythology, and fairy tales. Animal, vegetable (a potato!), and mineral mothers. A surprising number of insect mothers. Mother figures from religions (many Marys), and from several cultures, including pop culture. Historical mothers. Tragic and triumphant mothers. Murderers, martyrs, and midwives. Intellectual, artist and writer mothers. We have fairy godmothers, witches, saints and the all-too-human. Planets can be mothers, as can moons.

The diversity of mother figures can be said to reflect a multiplicity of actual motherhoods. The literary and art work in this issue illuminate figures of motherhood, in concept and in practice.

Jennifer Martelli and Cindy Veach

MER **Poetry Editors**

We are excited to introduce our exploration of mother figures with a poem written by a seventeen-year-old student who brilliantly spans the expanse of motherhood: from a tiny insect, to a mother bear, to a mother. In Zoe Smith-Holladay's poem, "mothership/hivemind," she writes:

> I am a mother, I think.
> I am a mother, but have little worries
> > of whether my children live or die.
> my little kid mind imagines a mother not necessarily as a protector, carer of a brood, but
> rather by observation of her grandness, power in relation to her meager children.
> > the queen of the colony: proud and commanding I stand parallel with sci-fi
> video game archetypes,
> > a gelatin mass of sustenance and the promise of offspring deliverance,
> > in charge of armies, million-fold—exoskeletons.

The poems in this issue of *MER* present a full range of archetypes representing our search for "mother."

These are poems that reflect real time and are loaded with historical and political weight. In Tamara J. Madison's, "Till Poem," Mamie Till's, face is "the sun. . . shining with pride and promise . . . ." Cynthia Atkins and Sarah Key honor the late Ruth Bader Ginsburg "in a lace collar, dispatching all the justice/she can muster with two gossamer wings" and as "never being afraid to be laced/with dissent." Sharon Tate, who was pregnant at the time of her murder speaks, in Kailey Tedesco's poem, "prenatal, all mine/to devour & yours now, too//umbilically."

Icons from pop-culture, movies, and literature are given emotional resonance in these poems when they are held up as mother figures. Their stories seem more complete. Maria in *West Side Story*, Aunty Em in *The Wizard of Oz*, Alice Notley, Denise Levertov, and Sylvia Plath all speak to the poets as figures of leadership, mentorship, and comfort. Nova, Charlton Heston's "silent partner" in *The Planet of the Apes*, who is given a voice by Beatrize Fernandez as she faces the State of Liberty at the end of the film, and claims, "That this child—my daughter—will be born with a voice. . . ."

The landscape—its flora and fauna—becomes a magical place of mother figures as well. Potatoes, delphinium, ladybugs, and the chili willow—thrive in this biota. Even the downright oddest of creatures is given beauty in Merie Kirby's "10 Interesting Facts about the Hagfish," where "the hagfish mother wraps around her eggs,/any feeling in her four hearts unchartered."

The poems in this issue are heart-felt and heart-breaking at times, like the hospice nurse in Joanne Clarkson's "Night Shift Nurse," where "no one is an orphan here," and as raw and biting as the anti-Semitic mother in Susan Rich's "Mother Figure," who dares to stroke the speaker's arm while crooning, "You people have such beautiful skin."

The depth of honesty, vulnerability, and skill in these poems moved us, and we are honored to be able to share them with you.

CONTENTS

FICTION

NONFICTION

CONTRIBUTORS' NOTES

MER

MOM EGG REVIEW

Vol. 20 - 2022

Zoe Smith-Holladay

mothership / hivemind

ever since I noticed   the space between me and the ground,
                    I always looked down:
my eyes tending to rocks, dirt, beetles,
                              downtrodden fruit and crushed leaves.
          earth in favor of the endless sky.
the morning after rainfall
                    a new beginning   in every neighborhood
     a visceral heave,   birthed from palmed handfuls of dirt.
the corporeal smell of grass and slick mud.
                              all the little bugs pack their bags, return to the
surface…
                    i wonder what they'd call it
          in earthworm tongue—-   this invertebrate
pilgrimage?
          rain marks the beginning and end
                    of their near-extraterrestrial arrival.
          maybe they recognized me
                              and the clay homes I would make them?
in the sidewalk dips and crumbly dens
          my dog always obsessively marked,
                    sinking her paws time after time into the earth….
          wanting to be buried   just like me.
     I was jealous of their dark, damp planet,
          Atlantis, sunken and forgotten,
          half-submerged in my backyard, quicksand—-
                    imagine a burrow, dim, damp, almost womblike.
yes, I could honor the worms.
                    take pride in them.
          but flies?
     I did not like the flies.
somehow, I could never force my motherly instinct for insects
          to extend to them.
                    the ability of flight made them selfish,
          imprecise and overconfident, too immediate, seething with gratification
                    desperate in every way: to exist. to fester,
copulate.

every lazy summer they wizzed between wildflower stalks in our dewy garden,
      feasting on snot in the wet noses of horses,
          driven into the barn by scalding, dry heat;
            I could only forgive their petty form
                with the thought of their promised metamorphosis.
        come fall,
              the flies will lay eggs
eggs hatch grubs
      grubs are wormlike, squishy;
        soft, vulnerable and really kind
          believe anything you tell them grub, sweet, little baby grub—
            "Did you know people eat them in South America!?"
        "where'd you hear that?"
        "they really, really do! I saw it on TV! I wanna try grubs too."
            "...Ew, honey, I don't think you'd like them."
         "how do you know?"
    "....I just do."
        Cherry Creek Trail was the biggest forest on Earth once.
I swore I'd catch a bear there,
        with a thin slice of King Soopers discount meat.
     here was my great contraption,   twine masterpiece:
a string that would hold the slab a few feet off the ground
              not too high
so we could come back on the drive home from school next week,
            see if it'll be gone.
      the relationship of
        the little kid
        to the small, trapped animal
          (whether a sick mouse, a ladybug, some goldfish
won from the Alabama County Fair or a few scatterings of ants scraped off the
pavement with a spoon into a plastic ant farm, complete with a little playground)
             —-"I bet they're like me, monkey bars are their
favorite!"
     is unrivaled in complexity.
          After all, how great is it to be six years old and say,
     small and bony and six years old....
       six years old, wearing just a bucket hat and a sweatshirt from an
airport she's never been to

holding a spider tied around dirty floss string——-six years old
'stubborn like her mother' six years old, crouching in a field and saying:
          "the ants? this is what they like. this is what they
want."
    I am a mother, I think.
    I am a mother, but have little worries
          of whether my children live or die.
my little kid mind imagines a mother not necessarily as protector, carer of a brood, but
rather by observation of her grandness, power in relation to her meager children.
    the queen of the colony: proud and commanding I stand in parallel with sci-fi
video game archetypes,
      a gelatin mass of sustenance and the promise of offspring deliverance,
        in charge of creature armies, million-fold——exoskeletons.
    running, hopping, unravelling in a crooked spiral
         all for a sliver of leftover Ritz cracker,
      a crumb fallen from the wrinkles in my dress when I stand up.
    maybe, for the ants, there is relief?
             ———in their surrender to complete powerlessness?
I go back at the end of the week, find the meat gone,
    my dutiful experiment completed, spotlight set, surely televised interviews are
imminent:
      there is a bear living in Cherry Creek Trail.
    I ask my mom if I can do it again with another slice.
she's tracing smiley faces with a stick
      crouched at the other end of the sandbar,
                   pauses,
      asks me to tell her about school that day.
        during the drive home
          my mom wonders aloud,
  "Why a bear? Couldn't it be something else?"
        this, I think smugly as I swipe through pictures of the scene
          with my stained, scratched-up Kodak camera
            is why I'm the scientist.

  these days I miss my children,
      wish I'd kept my baby teeth.
        when we went roller skating, Mom slips on her butt
   and, through laughter, Mama says, "she's falling! get up, fool!"

"fool! fool! fool!" I chanted, my teeth chattering at the cold wind,
always quick and curious, nosy and wanting to join in.

Mama pinched me,   saying, "Don't overdo it."

so I shrug, scooting over to the grass to go poke wayward

ants

asking them why they're not home yet——

that their mom is probably worried about them!

still rushing back to the anthill at dusk

carrying a piece of ham—   twice their size.

"Do we get to keep my wisdom teeth?"

I asked, clutching my mom's side as

we limped, fuzzy headed

out of the doctors office—

my shoulder nudged under hers

and a napkin tucked into my collar.

it feels like we're like one clumsy, merged body,

clambering through the door and out into the parking lot.

"Why would you keep them, babe? You don't need them anymore."

but I do want them.

even as my numb, gummy mouth tries to swallow, absorb the juice of an

ice pop,

i'm wishing for them, slumped in the backseat of the car:

the little ones that hurt the most

the ones I don't need.

every night that week,

i'm sleepy and sick, stuck in my sweaty, writhing body,

trying to divide myself into three sections like an insect:

head, thorax, abdomen.

my nose runs

and I wipe my sticky lips with a thin rag,

coated in saltwater,

and when I forget to fold it over once again

sticky blood gloms onto my

cheek

and dries at the base of my chin

until my mom comes back with fresh towels

and wipes it all away.

trapped in fleece blankets,

i'm small and miserable— —-

three sections: head, thorax, abdomen

and everyday I'm struck more by how much i want...

if I had the strength to open my mouth it would be to voice my naive demands,

all swirling at the center of my core like murky pond water.

i want my teeth back.

here I find myself in possession of a thousand fragments, spinal appendages all jabbing through the thick stuffing of layered comforters   in this moment,

in just a centimeter or two   I find there might be even a million pieces of me.

and I want my greed, my children of war back.

three sections: head, thorax, abdomen— —

and when my nose clears up, i want to smell the rain, the thunder again.

a million pieces, platelets   and not a single one mine.

"Mommy, where *is* South America?"

"I'm not telling you!"

" Why not?! Is it...down on a map, or up?"

"Why would we go there just so you can try and eat tree grubs, silly girl?"

"Aw, how'd you know?!"

"....I just do."

I love you, Moms.

POETRY: 1

"Cultures Rhyme" by Lawrence Bridges

Carolina Hospital

On Mothers: Paintings by Virginie Demont-Breton

Rough stones piled into a wall behind her, a bride in white
with veil, *Alma Mater,* sits, her infant on her lap sleeping,
no sign of his fate, but for a halo glowing against her breast.
She watches, her long lean arms open, a lace tent framing him.

Behind, an alcove, its flaked plaster bright blue. Above, wooden
cross planks carrying the weight of what's missing. At her feet,
yellow and purple wild flowers keeping her exquisite nature. Better
to summon the *Fisherman's Wife*, with firm arms and steady

calves hauling boys out of the sea, balancing over sharp boulders.
She harbors what's hers, like angels who scoop up Mary's house
in Nazareth away from invaders. On their way to Italy, they drop
bits over the lands. In every doorway we hang her metal plaque.

La Virgen de Loreto like the *Mother and Child* (frolicking)
in Waves, she guarantees our safety and that of our homes.

Leah Sandals

Bible

It's Easter-y. It's paradox. It's mystery.
It's bottled spiders and a bird that will revenge itself upon ya'll.
It's mummer's day. It's water, muttered. It's mother, uttered.

If I can never forget that I am not with you, a.k.a.
Gloriana-Una-Venus-Diana-Mary-Isolde-and-Isis.

For now we roam the sovereign words,
Making disso-natal queens of stomping steers
Taking pen to least papers, and making pets of pears.

Stand still, apostle-ettes, then lean in-to this:
Your mixed capacity for evil and for beauty,
For thrusting through thoughts of I and thou.

Somehow: ye goddesses, ye imperialettes, ye supreme-ines!
Ye potentates of fried potatoes, looting snack shacks
Sucking on lost chlorophylls, decayed skulls and sugared *salles*.

Is there room in these rooms – to be carried from corners?
This carrion we eat – is it marriageable?
This stone that we roll – is it the moon or marble cheese?

Melissa Studdard

I Dreamed Mary, Mother of Jesus

led the La Leche League of Houston, Texas.

She had the most magnificent breasts,
like little molehills that
people made a mountain out of.

When I asked her advice for rearing a child
she said, *don't tell them they're not immortal—*

if they find out, they'll die.

Her brain was bigger than a thousand books
and so powerful it could beat the internet at chess.

I told her all my problems.
I asked her all my questions.

She said *the distance around heartache
is shorter than you would think.*

When her son was old
enough to speak, he said her milk
was better than cookies 'n cream ice cream
or melted M&Ms.

And who could doubt it, when at her breast
eternity popped open like a broken

bra strap? Who could doubt the palate
of baby training to turn water into wine?

Rebekah Denison Hewitt

Baba Yaga As Ars Poetica

The oven is our mother—Russian Proverb

She scares the kids with her
cottage on chicken leg stilts
wiry frame, but mostly
her appetite—
                    triangular iron teeth.

The five-year-old asks me
to close the book
when she shoves the boy
in the oven.
                    Apple in his mouth
                    like a roast pig.
                    Her lips wet and glistening.

She comes to me
grinding mortar and pestle,
tells me to stop reading
the mom blogs
                    that promise joy,
                    home baked scones and children
                    who do chores.

She says, you'll be old
like me, and ugly, too.
What will you have
to show but an empty
womb. She piles
                    book after book
                    on my head and says,
                    eat these and see
                    that you'll never
                    be satisfied.

Kim Welliver

The Jeremiad of Isabelle Romée, June 1431

I taught you
we are animals:
salt and mud and sky-tricked eyes—
drays in the tangible grass, the low fields.
We are plowers, dredgers, gleaners,
turnip and bonemeal, we are the wormy apple,
a cabinet of stars inside.

I taught you bread making:
picking weevils from the rye;
grind and mill.
Our broad palms floured— knuckle and knead,
roll and pat, the yeast
loaves rising on the hearth—

I taught you to feed.

I taught you handwork:
wool and flax, beetroot for red dye,
onionskins for gold and for the purple
of old wounds. I taught you
needled stitch: sleeve-set and apron hem,
to love the feel
of goodish cloth.

I taught you to create.

I pressed your face to my breast
plaiting marguerites
in the rough silk of your black hair.
I taught you what we carry:
fragile as duck eggs pintucked
in our wombs like speckled moons
—something so filled with life
we must carry it
low, in the bowl of our bones

I taught you how the world unspools
within you—
a canticle in plainsong

I taught you to press
penitent knees to grit-flagged floors:

musk-wrapped, dusk-cluttered.
To mouth in mimicry
the unknowable Latin where Christ-windows
pour their colors on our veiled heads,
our tongues blessed
with absolution and the host.

I taught you to pray.

You left me to clothe yourself
in His name—donning
the fabric of men: steel and clock.
Stone tower and halberd.
Banner and blood.

You were my child
always reaching for the firefly's dazzle
for the whispers blooming like lilies of bone
like wings at your shoulder.

You taught me loss:
a darkness—immense and calling.

Every day I say your name
"Jehanne" "*God's grace* "
and fill my mouth
with ashes.

    * Jeremiad- a long lamentation or song of mourning
    Isabelle Romée was the mother of Joan of Arc

Meredith Trede

In the Eye of the Virgin

Believers see Juan Diego reflected
in her left eye. Come be close. Close
to the Virgin, feel the blessings of her eye.

The Dark Virgin, Guadalupe, appeared
on the hill where an alum water spring
led to the Nahuatl Mother Of Us All.

She-who-treads-the-snake will bless
our pain, cure typhus, loss of faith—
close your eyes. Now see the Virgin.

She bade Juan Diego *Build a church*
in my name. When the bishop wanted
proof, December roses bloomed;

her portrait rose from cactus cloth, now
pilgrims offer pain, pain the price
to be paid the church's Virgin of Dolor.

The Basilica Vieja sinks into the hill
of Tepayac, cracks shatter its stained
stone facade. The Basilica Nueva built

of resinous fibers, polyethylene, steel,
room for ten thousand. Her cloak above
a moving walkway in a bombproof case.

Come draw near her shrine. Buy
fragrant beads of rosewood, pulque,
plaster casts, enlargements of her eye.

Jen Karetnick

After We Move, We Learn about the Miami Supreme, a Matriarch Shrub

Masked and shielded in this home barely worn,
we nurse the gardenia budding by the door.

> We nurse the gardenia budding by the door.
> The neighbors, still new to us, call it iconic.

The neighbors, still new to us, call it iconic,
say it's as ancient as solitude and folklore.

> They say it's as ancient as solitude, folklore,
> its perfume enough to posy the block.

Its perfume is enough to posy the block,
alert the thieves. We nourish hope like a habit.

> Alert as thieves, we nourish hope like a habit.
> The blossoming is public though none of us are.

The blossoming is public though none of us are,
masked and shielded in this home, now so worn.

Mother Rapunzel

Sixteen Rubbermaid bins in my attic—
call it inheritance—foxed, unnamed
photograph faces; Snoopy Flying Ace
doll she kept, Nutley library back room,
where she glued pages back into spines?

Mice pepper bin lids with scat,
acorn shells, iodine-colored urine.
Spiders sling cobweb hammocks
from the ceiling; dresses dangle tags;

gift handkerchiefs yellow
behind cracked cellophane;
crazed Chanel #5 and Estee Lauder bottles;
46 hats she crocheted—never wore—

all she moated around herself—
as bulwark against bullets, thieves,
me—waits beyond a portcullis
of memories, one small opening
at the top of the pull-down stairs
I broke when last I emerged.

Mother, boxed up there,
send down the silken rope
of your braided hair.

Cynthia Atkins

No Fly Zone

for Ruth Bader Ginsburg

My son texted to say, "The fly probably got stuck
in his hairspray." Under the hot lights,
the fly was unassuming, but for two gorgeous
minutes, it was pure stagecraft.
          The lone fly laying eggs in the white
snow-storm of his hair. This was a Judge
in a lace collar, dispatching all the justice
she can muster, with two gossamer wings.
          My son is old enough to get a girl
pregnant. It could happen, just like that.
Our lives hang upside down, in the balance—
Fate on the laundry line of our dirty linens.
          A fly can land, spoil all your plans.
My son is studying to be a physicist—looking
At how things come into being, demand opposites.
          I thought the fly was on the TV screen,
so I tried to squash it, but it was on his real head.
I taught my son it was okay to have consensual
sex before marriage, yes I did, for fuck sake.
          But tell that to the lady
with seven children—opining to steal
the black robe of blind justice. On live TV,
the fly landed on layers of lacquer and plastic.
So toxic, he did not even notice. Every two minutes,
there are starving children being born.
          O Fly, build a colony in his ski-slope hair.
Let them procreate. *Let them eat cake.*
The son I birthed with joy, texted to say,
"The fly probably got stuck in his hairspray."

Dawn Terpstra

Ode to Delphinium

Mother declares you garden goddess,
swaying stalks spike azure-sky
like trumpets

heralding unspoiled beauty,
purple brocade.

Each spring you're a lady-in-waiting
for your reign
in the heart of the summer bed –

smooth royal-blue dolphin-shaped
buds swim
my 7-year-old blood – sweet-spurred

lobes dance painted with dawn's light
and shadow.

Ruby-throated hummingbirds
suckle nectar
from your suspended cups

rooted in the dirt of a mother's
dreams. Open-
mouthed, your lips, and white-

tipped tongue, everything you say,
brings her back to me.

Elizabeth Lara

Hera at the Bus Stop

My grandfather was a man of little conversation,
though you could say that he was Zeus and Mrs. Walton
was Io, because in some corner of their small town
they found a way to talk, and that day when my grandmother
(you could say she was Hera), all perfumed and hatted
and dressed to go to town, was waiting for the bus,
he must have been away at work or in his easy chair
playing cards, for he wasn't there to see my grandmother's purse

coming down on Mrs. Walton's head, scattering her hairpins
across the sidewalk and knocking off her spectacles,
or hear the gasps of passengers on the city bus
who gawked at the tangle of torn bodices
and sturdy shoes until the driver slammed the door
and drove on.

Tina Carlson

My Mother As Moon

Though I stormed the weathered

blood of her ancestors, I wanted milk
when I arrived. She promised food but

fed me iron. I starved. I dimmed into slack.

I wanted to be daughter and she said,
mother me. I was born in an asylum

of dawn, stream of light in my mouth.

I was transfixed by the pines
and all their green hands. On

ground blurred with dirt, quartz

gleamed like gristle. Now she nods out,
bent petals on stem, cratered leg crimson.

I tend the relics of her wounds.

Susan O'Dell Underwood

My Mother as Lethe, Goddess of Oblivion

Daughter of strife,
she had too many sisters to remember, anyway—
Dispute, Battle, Quarrel, Lies—artesian trouble makers.
Now we have medicated her to the saccharine shores of love,
but, sometimes we despair even now
 to distract her sudden storms.
She claws at the itch of her cheek the way
a cat twitches its aggravated tail.
A friend tells me she is still herself, somewhere,
way down deep, the tumble of all her moments
an icy dark star at the bottom of a well.
I see her move, though, in eddies and shoals,
unbridled in amnesia's white water.
She is the secrets fish say to the sleek muck on the rocks.
She is the doldrums, in a passive din
of pooling hot cerulean—blue stupor of her eye.
She is the muddy sluice where the hurricane pushed
its brackish argument against the bank,
the levee broken, the queen of the back-handed rivulet
after the earthquake turns foundations to sog.
She's the swamp croaking and croaking for lack of peace;
the river eating itself alive, channels flooded
and gorged beyond recognition.
She vexes the farthest buried grain of pebble,
damp forever at the bottom of earthen dam, plunging
and stubborn, faithful to the end
in her weighty refusal.

Elizabeth Sylvia

Unbind

Philip: Bind up your hairs.

****

Constance: I will not keep this form upon my head,
When there is such disorder – King John

Run into the marketplace with me, mothers of this world
for I have seen you weeping at the dry-edged river
and wading from the boats, dead children in your arms,

Run into the marketplace with me, mother, madre,
maman, madr, ahm, muter, mater, mama, mama, mama,
and we will take the pins out of our hairs and shake
our heads, and fill our silent mouths with hair,

Run in your bared feet to the marketplace with me
where we can beat the drums of grief until we open
fissures in the earth that swallow up the princes
who draw the lines our children cannot cross,

Flood the marketplace with hair of snakes
and words that cannot be choked back,

Shatter and rage and stomp until the maps
curl up in fists of ash because our hair
makes fire of the wind, and all around us knots
are come undone and birth instead of death descends.

Joanne M. Clarkson

Night Shift Nurse

moves from bed to bed
without turning on the light.
This is Hospice,
the final hours
when those who have already
passed come back,
wind through an opening door.

She embodies mother
after mother after mother
flawed or kind
eager or aloof
some in gowns of music
some with a touch of scent.

Do dry lips whisper *water*
or *mama,* cool at the rim
of a spoon?

She pauses by the restless ones,
dreaming of thunder
and the shatter of glass.
Replaces sharp-edged memories
with the gift still unwrapped.

My sister was my mother,
this one confides.
Then I will be your sister,
she replies, smoothing
the worrisome sheet

as the dying one raises thin arms
into empty air
near the embrace of morning.

She moves with the solace of shadow.
No one is orphan here.

Maria at the Window

They never made a *West Side Story II*
because Tony was dead and the last
time you saw me I was weeping over
his long, white body. The smell from
the smoking gun weaving into
my hair. The streetlight's puny glow
shining down on the gold cross hanging
around my neck.

Haven't you ever wondered what
happened to me? Did I ever sing
again, for instance? I didn't. They
took Tony's body to his mother, my
brother's back to Puerto Rico.

Sometimes I hum to the baby in
Spanish. I nurse her by the fire escape.
Together we can see past the roof
tops, with their little lakes of tar.
Everything has come apart, but I still
sew the stitches the way I was taught,
small and tight, holding together these
big American dresses.

Merie Kirby

10 Interesting Facts about the Hagfish

My child recoils at the photo,
the long pink-brown body curled like Swedish sausage,
the eyeless face all mouth and pushed out rows of teeth,
but he wants to hear the interesting facts:
>it buries itself face first into decaying bodies,
>secretes a thick protective mucus full of threads as strong as spider silk
>>and even finer than spider silk,
>produces liters of that mucus very quickly.

How does the hagfish live, covered in slime?
It does not. It ties itself into a knot,
pulls through its long velvet body to clean itself.
You're making this up, he accuses.
>A skull but no spine.
>Something like teeth but no jaws.
>Gills – and lungs – but no fins.
>When its single nostril is blocked with slime, it sneezes.

It is barely a fish.
Because hagfish skin can be tanned, used as leather,
people want to breed them in fisheries. But,
>hagfish will not breed in captivity.
>In captivity they live only half as long.

A fish so conditioned to wild survival does not care,
has not cared for 300 million years,
whether it disgusts or delights;
>deep in cold waters the hagfish mother wraps around her eggs,

any feeling in her four hearts uncharted.

Iris Jamahl Dunkle

Craft Talk in Which A Moon Follows

My dreams have become nests of violence.
　　　She says *we have such vast worlds within*
　　　us. Globes cut open – can't you hear the sound
of the bells reverberating off our

gutted curves? These days the night is shut off.
　　　Powered down. The moon rises over sea
　　　becoming large in its swollen moonness.
Is it following us? When my boys were

small, I'd drive them up the crooked roads of
　　　sleepy mountain until they'd let the world
　　　go. The days once again weighted with lock
down. *Are you wearing your cement slippers?*

My mother who is dead; who is an owl;
　　　who is a shade who flits through scree of dreams;
　　　still makes her complaints of the world known.
The poet asks *is everything nameable?*
　　　From this nest of waves. From this tepid fear
　　　bath in which we sit. Under surface
something rises—

Jane Zwart

Sailors take warning

Manually lovers tilt the chins
of those they mean to kiss

and Dawn, no different, angles
the mouth of this place

to face her, rosy fingers
adjuring from earth a jaw.

This morning the sun
has also feathered his bangs,

brushing the ginger cirrus
from his high forehead

into almost a pompadour.
I leave them to the young;

I know their mother.
She is the one I run toward

through the last of the dark
before the kids wake. I run

until the sky's eskers resolve
into rows of pink foam rollers

wrapped in her dun hair.
Each year we smolder less.

Romana Iorga

Witness Protection

with a first line by Mary Ruefle

From this day forward all plants
will allow me to rename them.
All will receive brand-new passports
and fictional lives. If caught and interrogated,
they will lie through their teeth
and refuse to cooperate. They will wither,
uproot themselves, splinter and burn
before they give me away.
When tortured and put to death,
even kudzu will be hailed as a hero.
Its children will scurry across the earth
like a leafy, life-giving pestilence.
Shaggy, the trees will grow at odd angles.
Unruly. Untamed. Spy on humans
and infrastructure. Smother the highways.
Picture this. In their wake, oxygen
fills our lungs to utmost capacity. Fills
our brains, our hearts. Hospitals become
obsolete. Airports, inaccessible. Also,
unnecessary, as the 100% oxygenated brain
has endowed us with the power to fly.
War belongs to the dark 21st century,
when all life teetered for one
agonizing political mandate on the brink
of extinction. Money is a curious thing
of the past. Factories and power plants
go green or fall into ruin. Many
are turned into art galleries. Museums.
Restaurants. Performance spaces.
My verdant godchildren wield
their edenic power: joyful, exuberant,
endlessly self-replicating. All of this
because of what language can do.
Meantime, I grow old and forget
their names, their complicated stories.
I only remember the green of their faces,
the rustle of many-fingered hands.
Each night, they tap on my window
and whisper. *You are the mother of all
vegetables*, they say. *You are the fruit.*

Colleen Michaels

Hera Shops at Whole Foods to Feel Alive

Contemplating the self-serve
soap bar, she dreams of a clean kill.

Here, you are allowed to cut your own,
so she portions herself a sliver

lemon verbena, sometimes charcoal
and tobacco, cruelty-free promises.

She pockets the sickle moon, struts
peacock style to the dairy and non-dairy isle

where with one side eye she besets a constellation
of allergies from nut milks to new mothers.

It is no coincidence that *Echo and the Bunnymen*
is in heavy rotation on her shopping days. Humming

about fate and killing, her nail pierces the flesh
of a pomegranate and then an apple.

She returns the produce cut side down to bleed or bruise
then scrawls on a comment card: "Pawed fruit. Do better."

When the cashier asks, *Prime Member?* She hears *Prime Number*
and responds. *Yes. Don't dare try to put me in a line with others.*

Libby Maxey

Talking about Clytemnestra behind her back

You would not have raised the knife
and brought it down
as she did;
there was time, more than enough
to think of consequences.

And weren't things bad enough already
for the House of Atreus?

You would not have laid down
tapestries, rich robes for him to ruin
with his feet—
for you to ruin in the bath of blood
to say there is not one good thing he loved enough to spare.

The theater, the heavy metaphor,
the irony—all in such poor taste.

You'd leave Cassandra out of it,
set jealousy aside (your own convenient lover standing by);
you'd spare the speech,
the corpse display, the proclamation
of your shameless vengeance.

Why sacrifice all sympathy
when you're a woman wronged?

But then, would you have shrugged and shuffled
like the Argive elders when you heard
what he had done?
Would you have held your child no better
than the blood to speed her father's ships?

When rage and grief have remade reason,
who's to say what any mother's hand might do?

Julia Lisella

For Elsa

Born below Domenica, she winds her story
through Florida, the Carolinas, until she's managed
a flood in Manhattan's Lower East Side, goes 6 inches deep on the Deegan
mashing through Connecticut's shore and fields
and now the rain she's brought
pelts against each of our windows in Massachusetts.
There is nothing better than the sound
of heavy rain, its muddled tone as it hits
sidewalk: flat; patio slates: sharp; garden patches: layered crescendo.
The dusty globe still sits in the corner of what was once my daughter's room
the screw that holds it on its axis loose again
even though no one has tried to spin it recently.
Still, the Earth loosens its grip from our efforts to tether it,
read it, follow our own paths inside it.

Alison Stone

Mother Tongue

Sure, it's my *mother tongue,* but just like a real mother
offers sweetness and then pulls the breast away.
Even another native and I
start communicating and then lose
each other in the ambiguity
of intention and sound.
Sometimes *I'm tired* means *I need to sleep,*
but more often means *You left dishes*
in the fucking sink again or *I don't want to have sex now.*
It can also mean *The virus in my blood*
woke up and feeds. Sometimes *tired* stands in
for *bored, discouraged,* or *victimized.*
And what does *victim* mean really,
when two people exhaust and hurt each other
trying to deepen their connection.
You've let me down, English,
with your vague syntax and ambiguous
clauses, your lack of heart-reaching phrasing
for what matters most. I wish
I spoke a more satisfying language,
one with words for kinship to a minor
character in a book, the melancholy
specific to holidays, or the sound
inside a seashell, which is not the sea.

Matthew Murrey

The Last River

My mother grew up on the river
and stares back at me now
from the other side
younger than a bride
and as surprised as we were
caught flatfooted by the floodtide.

I want to tell her everything
has changed since those days
you could dive off the dock,
those days she could cast a line
and catch something to eat, that day
the wind was blowing off the river
and she turned to see who
stood there taking her picture.

Now she is nowhere—
where the current is taking all
of us; that doesn't stop me
from talking to the water
or asking a fish for one more wish.

The river has no time
for fairy tales, comes sloshing in
the house and teaches us
how much silt and grief
we can bear. It's one thing
to see it on TV: somebody
spelling *HELP* on a roof,
or a car going under, hazard
lights still flashing and wipers
still taking swipes at the rain.

To be in it is another story,
like being a schoolgirl
in a photo from decades ago,
suddenly ghosted to where
the patio was, where water is now
chest high and catfish swim
between the legs of the drowned
iron table and its four heavy chairs.

Lara Henneman

The Infinite Memory of a Potato

I can hear my grandmother saying, *this will grow again if I bury it,*
holding a brown tuber by the green shoot poking through its dirtskin.
The potatoes grew by the back door lilies of the farm only I remember.
I went back a few years ago, invited in by the new owner, a cheery Republican judge.
Me (green dress, hungover) asking too many questions (goats, kitchen fixtures)
trailed by an ex (depressive, poet), after the wedding of a friend down the road.

This will grow again if I bury it. The farm will produce. My memories will return,
unbidden and brash, like life growing green out of a cellar tuber held in dark.

The missing of her has a shape like an exploded star. She is missing.
I farm stories, to remember: her tearing through the woods headlong on an ATV
in search of tree thieves who had taken a rare dogwood. She was out for vengeance
in her nightly patrols of the groves for weeks after.

She mostly ignored the herd of hulking black steer. I fed them apples over the fence
before she gave them to a farmer down the road for processing.
Her heart wasn't in it after David died in his sleep.
But the vitality is what she'd want me to remember. In the summer, she'd walk straight
into the pool in her linen trousers and straw hat to cool down and make me laugh.
The beds of foxglove and dahlias and iris, all spilling out into the yard. The wax beans!
The potato, memory says, the potato (starch, steady).
If I bury this, will it grow again?

POETRY: 2

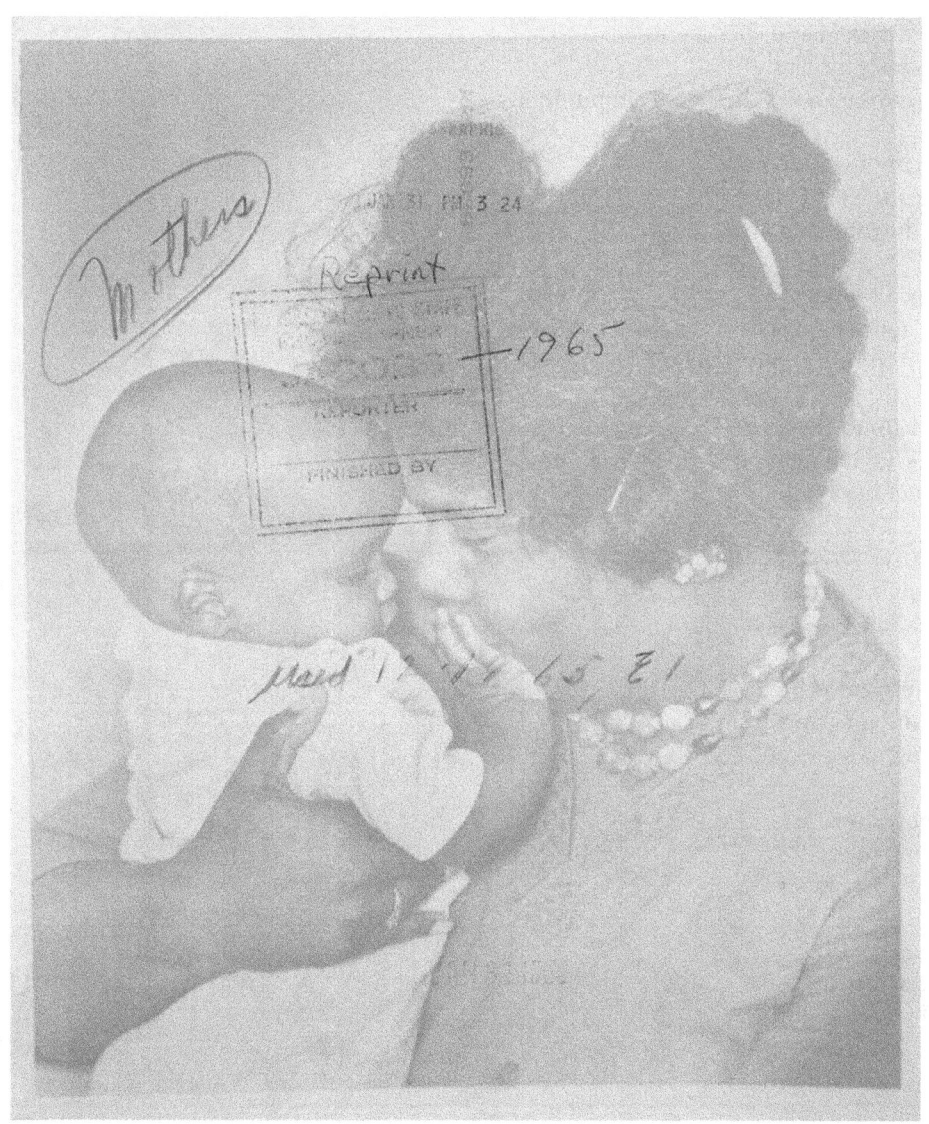

"Mothers" by Toni Pepe

L. J. Sysko

Paula

After *Paula Modersohn-Becker "Self-Portrait, Age 30, 6th Wedding Day,"* 1906.

With martial hand she secures
her breasts for battle
— everyone knows they store ammunition—

holds the fusillade back
surveys the field alone
Blue dragonflies dance

between bodies
in an apricot grove
Cutlery tinks from brothels

busy behind the lines
Here's lull enough
to water her horse

She paces forward despite
the pelvic floor ache
counts back to tasks

—razing an orchard
planting it again within
hearing its slow roots

winnow down
meeting maize
in the lower valley—

Craters pock
miles across
like nursery wallpaper

flocked and patterned
Picking their way
horse and rider

canter across a future piebald
and short
The period between wars

always belongs to mothers

Anne Owen Shea

Yellow Brick Road

Where does this road lead?
In a yellow circle back to you Em?

Back to the swinging porch door
that doesn't know whether

to open or close, back to the wind,
you calling my name waiting

for the sound to come back,
back to the red barn, you gathering eggs

in your skirt, to the kitchen
where you broke them open

in a hot pan, watching the life
that will never be, solidify

into a new body.
Back to the ghost of a house

that stands only in memory,
a house that has a voice

but no windows, a house
that was torn like a limb

from your body. I have taken
something from you,

if not your life. I have taken
the place where you rest,

the place where you turned
off the light. The land where

you planted seeds. I pulled
that world up, to see what

was buried beneath, the bones
of the dead, the roots of trees,

my mother.

Shutta Crum

Venus

There she is—pale Lucifer,
the morning star
(Not the mis-translated other
who fell from Heaven).
This one's firmly in place.

I raise a finger and touch
the cold glass through which I see
our companion planet.
And I wonder about the light
of a younger world—

before I birthed myself
from the salt and the silt,
might I have seen the daystar
flickering on the waves above me?

Might I have taken
that first painful gulp of air
as I caught her in the dawning?
Might I have called out
(as I sometimes do now)
for reassurance before day
donned its bright mask?

Might I have lain like a thing dead,
not knowing the miracles to come,
and awaited her in the dimming—
my Hesperus (Venus of the evening).

And there she is, a pledge I hold on to
in the rolling tilt of the night sky,
just past the tip of my finger—
lodged in the heart of this thing I have become.

Marina Carreira

Dollar Store Mary

Protect me while I drive away
from the screaming kids and sleepy wife,

the dirty dishes and laundry baskets,
the work laptop and unshoveled snow,

lead me down these icy roads as I drive
to the nearest Dunkin to get coffee and cry

in their parking lot. I need ten minutes
to spill myself, sit with the shadow grief's cast

over this year, its misty hands around my neck,
its smoky legs across my ankles so that

I'm choking, I'm tripping on death.
Holy Mother dangling from the rearview,

take this body to where there is no pain
or purpose, where I can lay like a diamond

against the darkness, shining and hardened;
hide me inside the song of a sparrow,

take me into outer space, where all I hear
is the sound of my own breath, catching.

RaShell R. Smith-Spears

A Writer Speaks of Lineage

My foremothers were magic.
Their nimble fingers squeezed syntax into cauldrons of rhythm
and rolled juju across pages that glared with our erasure;
they poured images into white spaces
defined by the narrowed lines of Black people's lives.
They touched history with metaphor, making charms to ward off lies.
As I wait before the page, inky wand in hand, I know
my foremothers were magic.

My foremothers were full of wonder.
I speak their names as incantations against the spell of invisibility:
Margaret. Toni. Gloria. Bebe. Leslie. Octavia.*
They have many clean words to say and unclean ones, too,
because they were conjure women unafraid
to work the root of racial weeds.
My foremothers were magic.

Why am I not as they?

*Margaret Walker (1915-1998), Toni Morrison (1931-2019), Gloria Naylor (1950-
2016), Bebe Moore Campbell (1950-2006), Leslie Esdaile Banks (1959-2011),
Octavia Butler (1947-2006).*

Jen Karetnick

Mail-Order Ladybugs

After we release you on leaves,
bas relief of gardenia bushes, to
climb in search of a fruitful aphid
dinner, we don't make a single

eager wish. We don't plead
for harvest, count the months of
good fortune coming our way on the
havoc of your stop-sign elytra, the

illnesses that you will wing away
just by landing on the afflicted,
kind of like a laying on of
legs. We deserve none of these

manufactured mythologies, though
now in the market more than ever,
Ophelia-ish, during this time of
plague when even hermits seek breaks from

quietude. Beetle named for the
rubied sorrows of the world's first
surrogate, small red cow in Wales,
the good God's animal, joaninha

(understood in translation as "little Joanne"),
Vaquito de San Antonio, there's nothing
we ask except that you drink from
xylobium's screaming mouth and eat

your fill of these invisible destructions,
zealous and bloodletting in your wake.

Cathleen Calbert

Girl Genius

for Sylvia Plath

Chaste as rain,
The moon coughed,
"Whiz kid, summer blonde,

You had your hands on God
When you thought of winning.
Talent can't save you now.

Woman of a blue planet,
Breasts swollen with muddy love,
Broken by the small tragedies

Of bread and baby mugs,
Why turn to me and beg reprieve?
Your nerves are shot.

Write dawn poems in blood
And signal to the difficult sun
You are ready to be reborn

As pure white light, then burn
Beyond belief in the paltry
Theories of your day,

Curl into granite and breathe
A litter of darkness to the stars.
I'll watch over your stone

As generations serve you up,
Poor dreamer." "Mother,"
I cried. "I will, I will, I will."

MaryAnn L. Miller

Between Earth and World

Mother has a peripatetic spouse;
she lets him back across the bridge every time.
She lies here full of fire and melted rock;
when she thrusts he runs from her passion.
If he were terrified, his feet would not move;
he'd have to stay and take his punishment.

Their hybrid babies are part dust and part mortar.
They're born in the space between natural and unnatural,
not that unnatural can't be good, or even stunning—
look at the cities from the sky at night.
Look at vaccines, shields against her bad side—
wild imagos on stained slides.

It's what he does with her milk that ruins the marriage.
The gap between Earth and World is runny with
chemical sadness— suckified draining—
collapsing her breasts like leaking implants.
We scurry between Earth and World to live, to heal,
to explain to children what is real.

Patricia Caspers

Hymn to Falling Sickness

> *Elizabeth Monroe was in such poor health that she and her husband had to remain in the White House three weeks after his Administration expired.*
> *— National First Ladies Biography*

Daily, rain gathers at spring buds while I am bled.
My home and body at once, purged
while doctors press mustard and fig poultices,
administer tinctures of Christmas rose and black hellebore.
It's no use. This, my life's secret:
I am a daughter of Lucifer.

Who else could be so cruel but Lucifer?
I pray and yet taste ash and iron in my blood.
Its scent blooms into chambers, bids me to secrete
myself away before my mind is purged
of sense, and to hell, again, I am borne.
For my pain, my dread, there is no poultice.

The servants ask after supper, and it shall be herbed poult
again. I care not for guests but seek in all moments *lucidité*.
Now we have finished; may I return to the land where I was born
safe from scrutiny until my father's loyalty was bled?
Now the congressional wives are purged
of my so-called snobbery, secrecy.

How am I to be anything other than secret?
Solitude is not a heart's true poultice,
as I have seen my father's countrymen purged
from our shores, but my tongue is stilled by Lucifer.
Here are the true leeches, unconcerned with my bleeding.
I pretend to be bored.

We shall leave behind a garden bursting with hellebore,
and the petals hold the reason as their secrets.
Behind closed doors, my husband's doctrine bleeds,
and only the future may be its poultice.
Perhaps we are all seduced by Lucifer,
and very few work to purge

his beetle from the ear; the others in a kind of purg-
atory of longing, or is it, in fact, hell?
Is this sickness an epilogue to revolution; Lucifer

among the colonists, an open secret?
Into this destiny *on tisse*
des regrets, and our banner bleeds.

It is not Lucifer, but men who purge
the plains, bleed and build, for some, an earthly hell.
I recant: My secrets die with me; *par conséquent*, my death will be a poultice.

Tamara J. Madison

Till Poem

for Mamie Till

We have buried you so many times,
sifted through files and notes,
slipped our fingers through cracks and crevices
to find some semblance of sense, justice, why-
praying it soothe us,
lay you finally to rest.
Still our palms and hearts echo
canyons barren.

Instead of sorting
puzzle pieces of your murder,
I choose to crown you, Mamie's baby, with a life poem.
Emmett, you amber-eyed, butterscotch,
Chi-slick, Black man-child with the tripping tongue,
I choose to write that bounce back
into your Midwest swagger
showing off before them country bumpkin boys.
I am writing you sliding into home base,
dusty Mississippi, Money painting your back side
bringing a cheering crowd to its feet!

Emmett, I am writing you:
a 14-year-old-grin of innocence,
wearing manish mischief for cologne,
lip smacking, trembling shudder
after the bubble gum first kiss
from a little brown/Black girl
where it is safe and sweetness
steals the blues from Mississippi air.
I am writing that crack in your voice
as hair sprouts on that landscape,
your body, your beautiful brown/Black
body skittering across Chicago
concrete beneath your heels
and Mississippi grass whistling
from the brush of your feet.

I am writing you running, Emmett,
back to the sun of Mamie's face
shining with pride and promise,

me writing/ you running
until you slam into her body, warm dough,
your face buried in the rise of her bosom,
your brown/Black face recording the song of heart
that followed you and you alone
because you are her only.

I am writing your first catch in that mitt,
recording your first swish at the hoop,
your first flitting fish on a hook,
your first words,
first teetering steps,
first fall, first crawl,
Lord, your first tooth and chew.

Emmett, I am writing,
you are crowning--
your first cry, your
first open eyes
yet womb-wet
bleeding Light

fearless, Emmett.

Tamara J. Madison

Soar

in memory of *Beloved* Toni Morrison

As a bird,
So below:
Our cerebral wings, sails,
Our calibrated souls, compass,
Our ancestral dowry and will,
Agency...

Sarah Key

Walking on the Beach the Morning After RBG Died
For Ruth Bader Ginsburg, Supreme Court Justice 1993-2020

Pre-history litters the beach
donned in dull brown –
overturned, tails pointing up,
down, sideways – horseshoe crab shells
seem to say we have come a long way
450 million years and counting

and we too have come far,
RBG in the lead, always first
to ask questions from the highest
bench, never afraid to be laced
with dissent

sticking up from the sand
the lance of a tail
bumps my thoughts into the umber
ready to joust,
what once was a rudder and tool
for flipping back up. Over and

over there are flips, backbends and
somersaults, until we end up
carcasses on the beach. I hold
one close to see how its shell
holds more colors than brown –
mottled and glaze-crackled,
slipper-shell-barnacled –
when held up to the sky
a strange translucence tells me

these carapaces are not carcasses at all
but creatures with new soft bodies
they've inflated with water
to split their old shells not to die, no,
for more space to live.

Abigail Templeton Greene

To Mother Like That

I longed to be young Maria Sanchez, played by Jennifer Lopez in the 1995 movie
Mi Familia. I longed to be that kind of mother.
The kind who wrapped her son in her rebozo and cradled him all the way from Michoacán,
Mexico back home to Nuestra Señora de la Reina de Los Ángeles (LA).
On foot, horseback, whatever it took to survive for the pulsing beat of family. I wanted that
thickness of story, to mother like a puma hunting in the night, like a vine weed creeping,
steady and unnerved. I wanted to be the hero like that,
to save my son from the drowning mouth of a river god, to harbor my children from the owls
of borrowed time who perch ready to swoop and swallow them whole,
heads-first.
I wanted to mother like a shield and find my children uncaught between dirt and riverbed,
released from the idea of borders and foreign land. I wanted to be the one
to free them from the dark tin of a hungry morning, and let a little sunlight touch their
chins.
A mother like Maria Sanchez, now that would be something to be proud of--
waiting with the light on, behind my apron a switchblade to survive.

Judith Sornberger

Isis's Apology to Horus

Son, I cannot do this anymore,
however much I've loved you
these 43 years. No longer
can I sail my paper boat
from myth to myth,
eyes focused for your fragments.

Let's face it, all this fishing
hasn't netted a single clue
for returning you to wholeness,
your birthright. So why
do I keep paddling

when the god of death
steals your voice, drowns it
in an underwater cave, and moans
through the remaining hollowness:
I wish I had never been born.

My eyes aren't so good anymore,
my arms aren't strong on the oar,
and oh, my son, my son,
heavy spondees pummel my heart.

But wait, what's that shell
that sparkles on the shore?
Maybe if I hold it to your ear
it will whisper the story
to steer you home—

not back to the mother's hearth,
but to an island born of a volcano
where you become the hero,
clawing through all that's been lost,
dredging up something
of yourself to treasure.

Susan Rich

Mother Figure

I'm thinking about ginger ale—extra dry. The bottle
wrapped in green and gold foil. The first bubbles
humming like a hailstorm of the mind.

Once, my boyfriend's Irish Catholic mother held my arm.
It was high summer, Duxbury, Massachusetts.
Your people have such beautiful skin, she cooed brightly

although I knew this was a butchering compliment—
and bewildering since she didn't know my sisters,
had never met my parents. She'd tasked me as her one,

her only Jew. *Beautiful skin,* the closest she
ever came to showing kindness, stroking my
forearm as the two of us sat hip to hip by the sea.

Two women—like extra-terrestrials, aliens
from separate solar systems—circling each other,
the ragged fault lines between us just facts

like the laws of no lobster, no ham.
That night she orbited my room—twice
to certify—no sexual relations with her son.

Jewish girls are easy, he'd informed me—
Sean…my one, my only…the house rocked
on the edge of a precipice. Downstairs, I heard

glasses clink and crash, as the patriarch sang
broken songs and smashed his fists on the shards—
while his wife sipped gin fizzes in the dark.

Patricia Callan

I'm So Sorry Sir, but Rockport is Actually a Dry Town

A temperance crusader in a patchwork shawl,
Hannah Jumper led the girls through town.

While their husbands pissed pennies against the bar,
the kids squeezed into last year's shoes.

What could they do but fight— hack away,
until the barrels screamed for mercy and the streets ran with rum.

Seven score (and four) later, I'd regale my
tables with the tale but disappointed tourists,

unable to ply their wives with wine,
were unimpressed by their teenaged waitress and her soda water.

I measured Hannah's elderly virginity
against my own adolescent creep past it—

Kissing on the wall beside honking cars
and that cook that would untie my apron when my hands were full.

His mother slapped me once to break my habit of chewing my necklace.
No one ever slapped him, as far as I know.

Hannah would have- would have rolled him over a barrel
and spanked him before taking her ax to his unsavory smirk.

Hannah didn't suffer fools.
Hannah was a warrior.

But I *do* wish she had taken my tips into consideration.

Natalie Solmer

Reading Alice Notley

after stepping into Alette's fetal
subway car, I laid on my broken, blue

sofa and dreamt I bled out a heart
like when I bled out the big clots

after having both my sons.
I could stagger, walk

leave behind a bowl of blood
on a bedsheet.

In my dream I fingered what was formed
but not fully—the heart was like the head

of a tiny tulip. My fingertips flittered
its petals. There is someone

I'm done with.
No heart. In the dream

I held a heart connected to no vein
and I recited something that came from

nothing or maybe the subway car:
O, upheaved plateau of eye!

Or was it I?
O, upheaved plateau of I

I guess I should grieve you
but only my body gives you away.

Julie Cyr

Leda in the Gulf

after the painting by Adam Miller

When Deepwater Horizon exploded,
Leda's baby latched on
as the waves became slick,
the film refracting light
into a false rainbow.
Leda sat naked on a rock
while the swan died,
oil cleaving to feathers
as pollen clings in spring.

The arrogance of looking
for the love of your life, adrift.
Leda looks in the smallest places –
the shell of a hermit crab
or under a pebble,
the vast places taken up
by spillage and underwater plumes.

Leda sat and nursed her baby
until her milk ran dry.
Even a goddess can't breathe grease.
Her head settled into the water,
her baby bobbing like the swan,
the sea lubricious with oil and fire.

Margo Taft Stever

MIT Poetry Workshop, 1969
for Denise Levertov

At 3:00 a.m., four hundred cops breached Harvard's University
Hall with clubs, helmets, visors, cans of mace. Pushed one
hundred of us into a hallway, crushed and tear-gassed us.

Close to seventy-five injured, one ankle shattered; she would
never take a normal step or run again. In paddy wagons, they
hauled us to the Middlesex County Jail—boys in one cell,

girls in another. In your MIT workshop, you told us
we would meet only in our apartments, never in classrooms.
You wanted to teach poetry to scientists. We demonstrated

against the Vietnam War. When poets possess the ability to write,
you told me, they do not own their gifts any more than people
own land or animals. Poets are vessels from which poems

emerge. Using a payphone, Mark and I called you from
the protest against Hayakawa during his speech that January
at Northeastern University. You were giving a poetry reading,

but you didn't want to miss the protest; you brought several
attendees to join the demonstration. We witnessed you emerging
from the subway stop, your voice raised against the cops

closing in, your arms waving through tear gas. Police bludgeoned
the young men who accompanied you and dragged them away.
Later, you looked over my photos of the Harvard Strike to find

one for your new collection, *Relearning the Alphabet*. You thought
the image of the students looking out at students looking in
the half-moon window resembled runes of an unknown language.

Tina Carlson

Until I Could No Longer Fly and So Became a Map: (Pegasus)

Just before prayer, my mother slept
in a sea of snakes, her holy, her grist,

bone meal and blood. I swam between her
continents of heartbeat and lung. She was throat

pulled open and slit, her quieted voice
made me winged and I fled from that nape,

I flew. Through clouds small as fists I rose,
serpents taut as a tongues on my back.

Cinched by men who wanted the sun,
I rode them out the stone of her gaze.

My mother's song a hover and flame, in barracks
on the ground. I wanted to gallop and nap,

wanted to feed at her feet. How she bled down
the stairs like pomegranates. Her hands rising

in prayer, before the death of my birth: fetlock
and dock, withers and croup.

My shadow a streambed, my glass into stars. Old
now, I flank a map. I am muzzle of plains.

In these days of war, rivers glint
my haunches. I drink from oceans

of the missing and yearned. I am hobble
and bruise in the dark dirt. My mother, my maker,

now daybreak and flaw. Smoke and flower
flush-plucked out of her gaping hands.

POETRY: 3

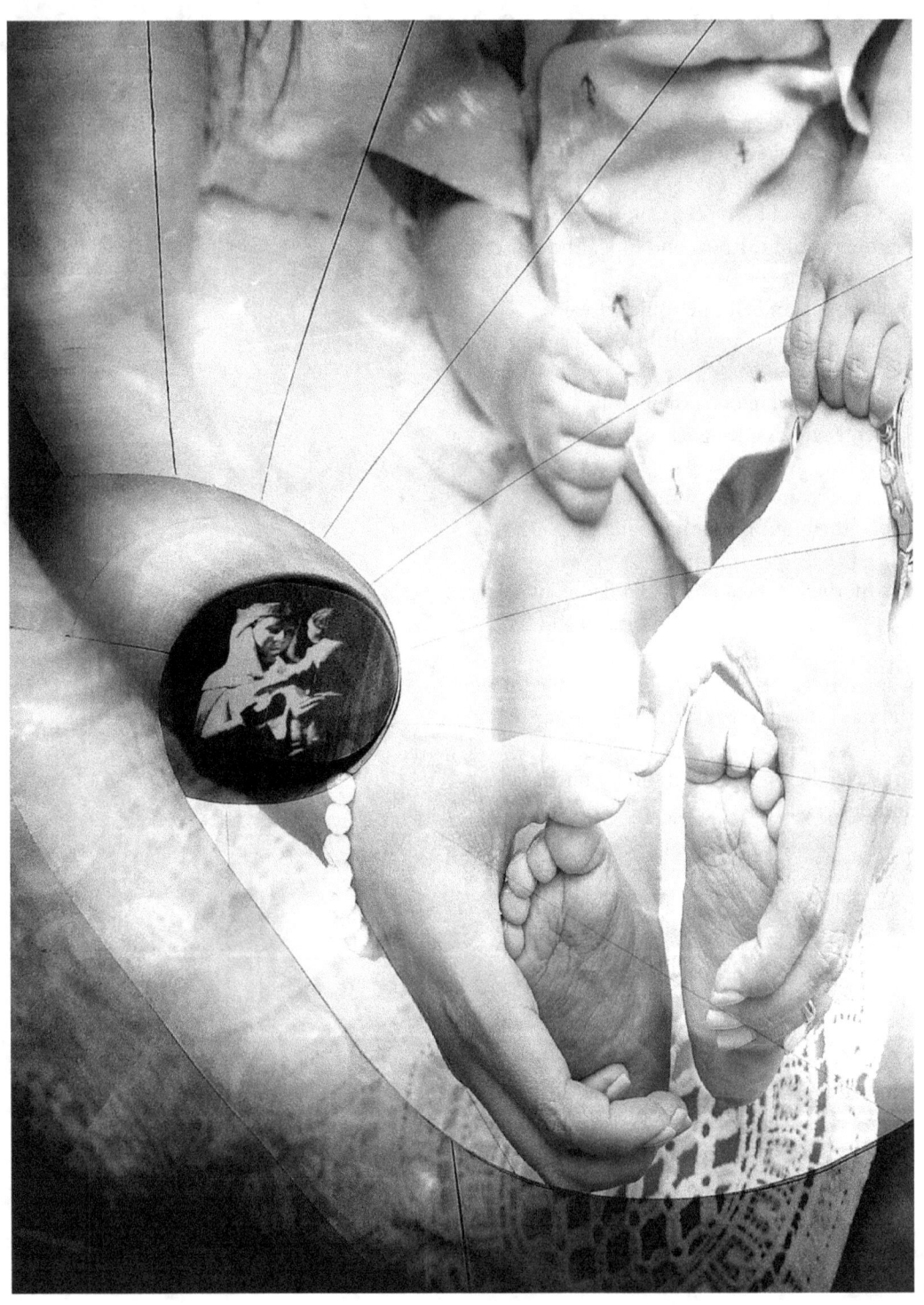

"Holding Pattern" by Karen Boissonneault-Gauthier

Chelsea Fanning

Virgin Mary as Teakettle

Praise be to you, spattered
with chicken grease and garlic fat,
the cerulean of your enamel
like a blue mantle,
sanguine in its austerity.

Down your throat holy faucet waters
pour, impregnating your belly before
you're cast into the flames.

Blue light caresses your sides
heats up the sea inside you,
tempest waves rising to a fever
until you scream in ecstasy or terror.

Beatriz F. Fernandez

Nova's Voice

final scene of The Planet of The Apes (1968)

I watched Taylor stumble in the surf
cry out to the skies, prostrate himself
before the fallen figure of a woman,
a spiked crown on her head,
her arm raised as if to touch the sky—

His grief a mystery, but I had no voice to ask—
Was she a goddess whose worship he had led?
Was she a mighty ruler from the old world he had fled?
Was she the symbol of a mother he had lost
in the faraway lands where he traveled?

Perhaps a remnant of the old world
where humans had voices, as he does
where women had voices,
to sing, to pray, to scream—

The dim sun set on his slumped shoulders
as the waves crashed against his idol.
I felt the first faint flutter of life in my belly,
pressed my hand against the stirring.

And I knew, I knew with a certainty
that now grows stronger each day,
that this child—my daughter—
will be born with a voice.
In a night full of broken stars,
I will hear her cry out my name.

Shutta Crum

Demeter and the Corporate Good Ol' Boys

the oil in the grain went rancid
the bread rose, gall-like and bitter
she served it anyway
the dust in their mouths
the taste of Demeter's revenge

raped by Zeus, the CEO of the whole shebang,
her daughter taken to the underworld—
given gladly by her father to his brother Hades

but soon, the gods got to thinking their grain-mother
was overworking this whole grief thing
why let the crops die, the fruit wither

come home, the corporation's good ol' boys said,
straightening their crowns and golden wreaths,
clicking their pens and looking efficient,
there's work to be done, they said
we'll send you a train ticket

why dress in black, why wander
without an oven to call your own
Persephone was a ripe young thing
she's fine—even ate some pomegranate seeds

look, here's your daughter now—hold her
while you can, let the green world flourish
and the bread be sweet again
you won't have to say good-bye for . . .
shall we say six months?

that-a-girl

Genoa Yanez-Alaniz

The Burden of Mary
(or When I Purge I Am forgiven)

I place the pills onto my tongue
each dissolves

as I fold in contemplation
falling holy to my knees

I rise and my confession
blooms where my wrists bleed

Seven stripes stream as rivers
gathering at my feet

Where a mother lays her skin
fatigued and split in three

The pills remain my rosary beads
I will swallow the hands of Mary

Katie Manning

Dear Carol,

Do you mind if I write you the love poem
I'd write to you after your death while you
are still alive? You didn't know at the time,
but you once brought my faith back to life.

In a tiny room to the side of our college's
cafeteria, you gave a talk on Julian of Norwich.
"God is also our Mother," you said, serving
as doula and midwife, inviting me to breathe.

Now Julian sits between us in the form
of my four-year-old son, eating oatmeal
and blueberries, coaxing you to bring him
more cookies from your office, shouting

in wonder at the surfers we can see
from this ocean-view room, reminding
us again that God is always our Mother,
writing *fear* in the sand to wash it away.

Tamara J. Madison

Rise

At the billow of daybreak,
BigMama blesses breakfast,

> *Rolling clouds, my coffee*
> *Shooting stars, my tea*
> *Rattling bones, these biscuits*
> *Peace freed*
> *And be…*

Shikha Malaviya

Naming/Nāmkaran

Aai,
    Is it really true?
        That being named after a river
            is bad luck, a turbulent life?
                Are all women rivers then?
        And tell me the story again
      of how I came to be
    a paisley in your belly
why you named me—
    daughter of the blinding sun
        sister of the lord of death
           tumbling down to earth
              to meet her blue beloved
        how I was born the same day
      as a goddess riverine
    whose holy drops
the priest sprinkled on my forehead
    eleven days after my birth
        introducing me to this world
           whispering into my ear
              Yamuna, Yamuna, Yamuna
        a contract signed in water
      a girl's fate sealed

Note: Anandibai Joshee was born on March 31, 1865 in Kalyan, Maharashtra, India, on the auspicious occasion of Yamuna Jayanti, a day commemorating Hindu Goddess Yami's descent to earth as a river.

Nāmkaran (Sanskrit): Hindu naming ceremony typically performed eleven days after a child is born
Aai (Marathi): Mother
Blue beloved: referring to the Hindu God Krishna
Yamuna (Hindi/Sanskrit): A girl's name derived from the Goddess Yami, daughter of the Hindu sun god, Surya and the goddess of dusk, Sandhya, and twin sister of the god of death, Yama: Yami represents life and together with her brother represent creation; the Yamuna is the main tributary of the sacred Ganges river in India.

L. J. Sysko

Everything's Elegy

Swallowed— winging my goggle eyes around inside Jupiter's tyranny—I feel like Metis, or her
daughter: Minerva—in birth throes, delivering myself from skull-thick cruelty.
I've been crying a lot lately, in traffic while driving from grocery to home and vice versa.
On occasion, I arrive at optimism: press the sunroof button, goddess divine, and rise
like a middle finger into the weather! Let whatever pathetic fallacy brews outside be thine!
On other occasions, I am:

Ismene—left-lane-proceeding, mumbling in retrospective rehearsal. Shoulda said this, shoulda
said that, or:
Cordelia—cast in road trip movie, gripping the steering wheel within a skeletal chassis,
pantomiming freedom on a lurching gimbal.

And to protag is different from what anyone supposed, and weepier.

I've been crying facing people whose business isn't mine. Choices are few and actually binary:
to mute awkwardly, let storm clouds amass on my face's green screen map, or speak anyway
and into the wind like a hurricane correspondent, gales lashing my cheeks and whipping my
hair, one lightning flash burnishing another, until I remember I'm neither meteorological nor
mythological, just a person whose hope outpaces reality no matter how fast she guns it off the
lights or how many groceries spill and roll around the back: daredevil pickles packed in glass
perching with eggs on the precipice.

My optometrist asked, this lens or this one? This one/this one? How about now? Until the
entire proposition dissolved into equal parts panacea and failure. I cried, but he mistook my
apoplexy for dilation. I kept daubing with my fisted tissue, squinting into the blur
beneath a gargantuan E
spread as if pinned on an entomologist's board. A common housefly,

Metis had 3,000 simple eyes mounted together at the front of her body—figureheads on the
ship of Futile Vigilance.
There's no Ship Name for Jupiter and Metis, for what a hack without compunction will do to
a Titan, let alone a myth.

Up Route 202 and back again, I pass a woman I used to know—her car coming, mine going—
and though she doesn't see me, I see her:

a bust above the dash, shining like marble in a museum rotunda.

Jo Angela Edwins

Eve

How many words
contain her name—
even, as if
she had an even
chance. *Prevent*,
as if her sin
weren't pre-ordained.
Of course, *every*,
as she was the mother
of it all, dark
and light, yes,
even the serpent,
her writhing child,
the birth of her
undoing. Who
can blame her, not
trusting the men, the
father who commands
without explanation,
the mate who complains
of the pain she left
in his robbed breast?
The prophet had him
sounding thankful,
proof the prophet
thought himself
a man. Any wonder
she identified
with a thing soon to be
forced to crawl
each day on its belly?
But that's not right.
She proved strong, as are all
things built of bone.
How else explain
her choice to leave
paradise (make no
mistake), to bring
a beautifully flawed
world into being?

Who else but this
stiff-backed woman,
caught in the midst of
both *never* and *forever*?

Joanne M. Clarkson

Mokosh

is the durable Slavic goddess
with her altar of breast-shaped
stones pried from the garden
along with weeds,
random at the seashore,
one with a barnacle nipple.

No one ever sculpted this Venus.
No one pin-pointed her constellation.
She is earthy
and thirsty.

Named for moisture. Her feast day?
Any day it rains. Her theme song?
The wail of a difficult birth. Salvation
is in her large, calloused hands
and the profile of a bosom
under bib overalls.

The only woman honored in the Slovak
pantheon with its scant written
tradition, Mokosh is patron
of writer's block.

She's the teacher whose ample chest
was at eye-level when I mistakenly
called her Mama in fourth grade
and the whole class laughed.

The one who gave me, not daily
bread, but a weekly
vocabulary list, words I collected
into small altars,
ovals and flat pre-teen jewels
with their inspired rain.

H, as in Womb
Now Sarai was barren, she had no child. (Genesis 11:3)

As in, I keep mine
Blank

As Buddha's mind
As a bench

That's useful only
In its emptiness.

A fallow field.
A space to pitch a tent

Then pack and leave.
As in the darkness

Of Pandora's box—
Hinged shut. As in silence.

Foreign to the tongue. Beloved
Of the ear.

Genoa Yanez-Alaniz

Severing Maria

In the photo she texted
her excessive and carmine uterus — sits inside a sterile dish
Her motherhood noduled — dead-fleshed and disposed
severed limb of life once divining deity of Coatlicue
— vigil of body and earth

A newborn cries red-faced and gasping for that first burst of sacrifice
served survival at mother's breast — her enduring gift of sustenance

Celebrated memory of gilded crown — of quinceañera princesa
Curious reach for that alluring and elusive gasp of pulsing crimson
honeysuckle bud and drip — piqued angel shape of sweetness

Maria, spirit and embodiment of Second Woman
Flower-temple of sex, beauty, and motherhood
emblazoned on your chest
(Xochiquetzal)

Cheryl Boyce-Taylor

The Grand Days of Noho Star
for Kathy Engel

Dear Kathy I miss our poetry brunches
at Noho Star
our talks on MFA programs
children spouses mothers finances
manuscripts submission guidelines—
I miss our San Pellegrino flat radish onion and avocado salad

at Noho Star we enjoyed
fried onions in a spicy mango chutney
it was there that I tried *Blue Moon* beer for the first time
with two orange slices
she gave me not one but two orange slices
and who ever heard of Mexican pizza with raw eggs on top
or fried shrimp with garlic eggplant

on other days a white eight-seater bench
on Lafayette Avenue near the window
held our joy after readings
after classes after book launches
where we sat for hours sipping drinks and laughing loud

then that time the clumsy white boy spilled deep red Chilean wine
on my new suede jacket
on my mother's beige antique hat
Golda held me back I almost fucked him up
because he refused to give his name
and hid in the kitchen rather than apologize

it was at Noho on that fall Saturday evening
that I fell in love with Kathy Engel and her two beautiful daughters
we set out on a journey of writing poetry and keeping each others secrets
I think of you Kathy and our beloved Noho
every time I order garlic eggplant and curry fries
from the bodega near my corner.

Katherine Gaffney

Mary (crater)

Imagine my bump snuggling
you, Mary —
I'd magic the moon into a cap
for my belly.
A moon cap for the moon my middle
has become. A cap
named Mary. A merry cap marked
by a sea of gray.
I know *Mare* is sea, but I hear a horse
willed and writhing
over the moon's surface without
regard for its name,
Serenity. Just as no Mary makes
choices based
on affiliation to history's Marys,
a horse running
cares not for her bloodlines.
Watch the craters
of her nostrils grow, who knows
she could be carrying
now, running with a foal in the making
and not know,
or she might think *here is my chance to teach*
in a way *I will never*
teach again, just as crowning my bump
with you Mary,
will have this child feel the weight
of something so absurd
she will never believe it until I crown
her again and she feels
the exact weight again pressing on her.

Pam Bernard

The Mysteries

There's some human truth to them,
the mysteries—how, for example, my mother
made magic each day as a kitchen aid
in my elementary school cafeteria.

We'd watch her from behind the glass
that kept us hungry kids at bay as we
waited for the lunch bell to ring.
She'd line up slices of white bread
on her long wooden counter,

dip her wide knife into a vat
of peanut butter, and with one swirl
cover each slice edge to edge,
right to the crust, then
began again with jelly.

Up and back she'd go, now
perfectly placing on the top slice,
cutting corner to corner
and centering the sandwich
on a square of waxed paper. Then,

with a skill I still cannot fathom, she
wrapped each with such speed
and precision that the hungry kids
would grow silent—and made
a stack so high it would surely
topple, but didn't.

Kailey Tedesco

Sharon Tate Suns by the Pool

after photos taken by Jay Sebring & Wojciech Frykowski, 1969

arching all my ripe, i let the sun
swell its way into me, un-line

my eyes, my signature cleopatra—
i enjoy this newest incarnation.

in my yellowest of moods,
i could never have predicted

an infant within me, mittens first
emerging. there's something

about the sky, harnessed
like a dog-walk, star-slathered

lacquer glittering against
my fingernails as i read

horoscopes by the pool.
there has always been something

about the sky. i swear i see
stretch-marks across it,

bolts unraveling from
a hand with power. at that night's

restaurant i eat
up all the electricity,

pure heat
scalding everyone's plates

& i'll keep eating the light
bulbs & their lamps—

prenatals, all mine
to devour & yours now, too

umbilically.

Richard Stimac

Visiting Mother Jones's Grave
(Union Miners Cemetery, Mount Olive, Illinois)

Incus clouds change hues: soft coal to hard lead.
Lightning strikes. Furrows flood with summer rain.
Beneath these plains, a cross of empty mines
Supports the country's heartland. My car whines
Down gravel country roads. The tires throw stones
And shake off dust. I hear a distant train.
I've come to try and honor bygone dead.
They buried Mother Jones in Mount Olive.
A cracked obelisk marks her resting place.
No one visits her tomb. She will not rise.
I ache for her faith in progress. But lies,
Here, history, yet unseen, fills this space
Around her grave. "Her boys" no longer live.
None will unearth these wrathful Irish bones.

Francesca Bell

Proofs

When the Holy Spirit entered her, Mary was a room made dark
by the first sliver of light. Once void, she remained ever after
devoid of:

     the empty that exists when something has been taken away.

No woman who had lain after fullness and felt love trickle out of her
would have said, *Let it be done to me according to your word.*

Had she felt life unfurl inside her, or a child tear its way out, and then waited,
a wide wound, as her body closed, she would never have said,

*Give me the child already nailed into place, destined to run with the scissors of His life
pointed up. Let Him breach like a great whale beneath the dome of my stretched-taut skin
and force His way out of this slit husk. Behold.*

I am the handmaid of the Lord, His strange carapace.

The useless shell that cannot save Him.

Merie Kirby

The Star Refuses to Do One Thing at a Time

The neuroscience people now insist we actually cannot multitask. We think we can, but really we move our attention from one task to the next and back again in microseconds which only feel like they overlap. And yet, here she is again, my tarot card shadow, the card I am most likely to pull from any deck. The Star pours out two pitchers at the same time, kneeling to the ground, one foot in water, naked and unconcerned that we can see her soft belly, intent on her multiple tasks. Does she ever reread her grad school recommendation letters and try to imagine who she used to be? Does a scar arc across her belly, too? Does she stay up until 2am to feel alone, to read without interruption? How long did it take her to master her child's new name, new pronouns, to firmly correct friend and stranger? How often does anxiety flare along her nerves, contracting her limbs to her chest? Maybe she pretends not to see the dust that makes her wheeze because if she isn't going to be allowed to multitask then some things will need to remain undone. It isn't magic, she says, it's math. If a microsecond can be divided, it can be split open, another tucked inside, again and again, time unfolding within each microsecond, until believing she can do two things at once becomes doing. *It's easy*, she tells me, *you keep one foot in water, one foot on land, you pour with both hands, the pitchers never empty. You're naked when you know who you are.*

Ingrid Andersson

Nova Stella

I knew from the out-of-the-blue
lull that can befall hard labor,
bestowing sleep,

that she was fully dilated:
I pronounced her *complete.*
The woman roused,

turned dilated eyes to me
and said—with blinding
depth and more

love than I have ever seen—
No one ever told me that before,
and reaching down

through a burst and flash
of milky caul,
caught a

daughter.

B. Tyler Lee

Chili Willow Denouement

The chili willow didn't know until I told her that *denouement* emerged from the French verb for "untying." She asked her name in French, but it wasn't as electric as we'd hoped: *Le Chili Soule*. But *soule* sounds like sole, like solo, which is what she is: Her savory dust powders the ground year-round, red against green shoots in spring, murder in the snowfall. Marsh wrens too afraid to nest, honeybees too coated to pilot themselves in her shade. Her brutal splendor blankets my house when the wind kicks, and I must cook my way out. We make curries, we make moles, we make *petit fours* with surprise violence inside. She eats from sun and roots and not my spoon, of course, but we're both a little less alone.

One night, asleep after jambalaya, I hear rapping on my window. A slim January branch beckons me to lift the sash. When I do, she curls in, lifting my gown until she finds what she's looking for. She presses the secret knot behind my bellybutton, and out she falls. Not *she* the chili willow—*she* my daughter, a rough fruit I've held within me all these years. "It's time," the chili willow whispers. I gather her berry body and plant her in the rusted ground. *From blooddust to blooddust*, I repeat, until I'm sure she's soil and *soule*, until she feeds the chili willow. Until I'm certain everything I eat out of necessity and isolation will be filled with her ending, with our savage love.

Ingrid Andersson

Phalaenopsis

Moth
is what an apostle
of Linnaeus named it.

But at this kitchen table
in this liminal hour, I'm tired
of men's takes on nature.

And Linnaeus, old spy
in your hothouse of flowers,
you might have reconsidered

the tendriled upended genus,
the profane yet prayerful
shape of it, if

just before dawn
you knelt, as a midwife
or a lover does, before

the rising body of a woman.
Her epiphytic mind, her
singular surging muscle

and orbed gynecoid hips,
coming to a head
between tendriled lips

and radiating:
Promise.

Kristy Webster-Gonzalez

Mother Jezebel

You were the face of my nightmares:
A grotesque expression,
painted lips,
a plunging neckline,
and garish red hair.

I thought you were poison,
but the dogs drank your blood-
I learned from the yellow, red-lettered
Book of Bible stories for children.

When pictures taught me
everything I knew about God and prophets,
Jesus and whores,
and *you* were the worst of them.

I thought I knew you.

But for a moment in my twenties,
I grew into beauty and when the hem
of my black dress edged above my knees,

Two men in suits, Bibles
in hand, led me into a dark room
where your name pulsed in the walls.
Your name became my name,
"*Jezebel, Jezebel woman,*"

The elders stood above me,
stared down and I stared with them
at my naked knees,

My bare legs tempted men,
they said, how cruel of me,
Think of wives and sacred unions,
and pulled at their ties,

And I whispered, *Jezebel,*
but your name tasted different
on my tongue,

I swallowed my spit,
sucked your name into my belly,

Now, when I breathe,
I breath fire.

Can you believe that once
I feared you? Devil woman.
Temptress and Reviler.

My apologies, Mother Jezebel,
next time, I will break your fall
with the soft of my lap.

Meg Yardley

Heliosphere

To travel beyond my mother's bubble
of brightness – where comfort
tethered me – I endured pressure
and shock jarred my bones.

Crumpling and re-forming
under blasts of radiation,

I sighted new planets.
I grew big with starshine.
I ate the interstellar medium for breakfast.

Back home, my mother's magnetic warmth
extends out, holding all the planets, offering
unconditional shield against cosmic rays.
The solar wind ruffles my hair. As if warmth

were a sedative to fight against, I push myself
away, out of orbit again.
I breathe in shards of stardust.

FICTION

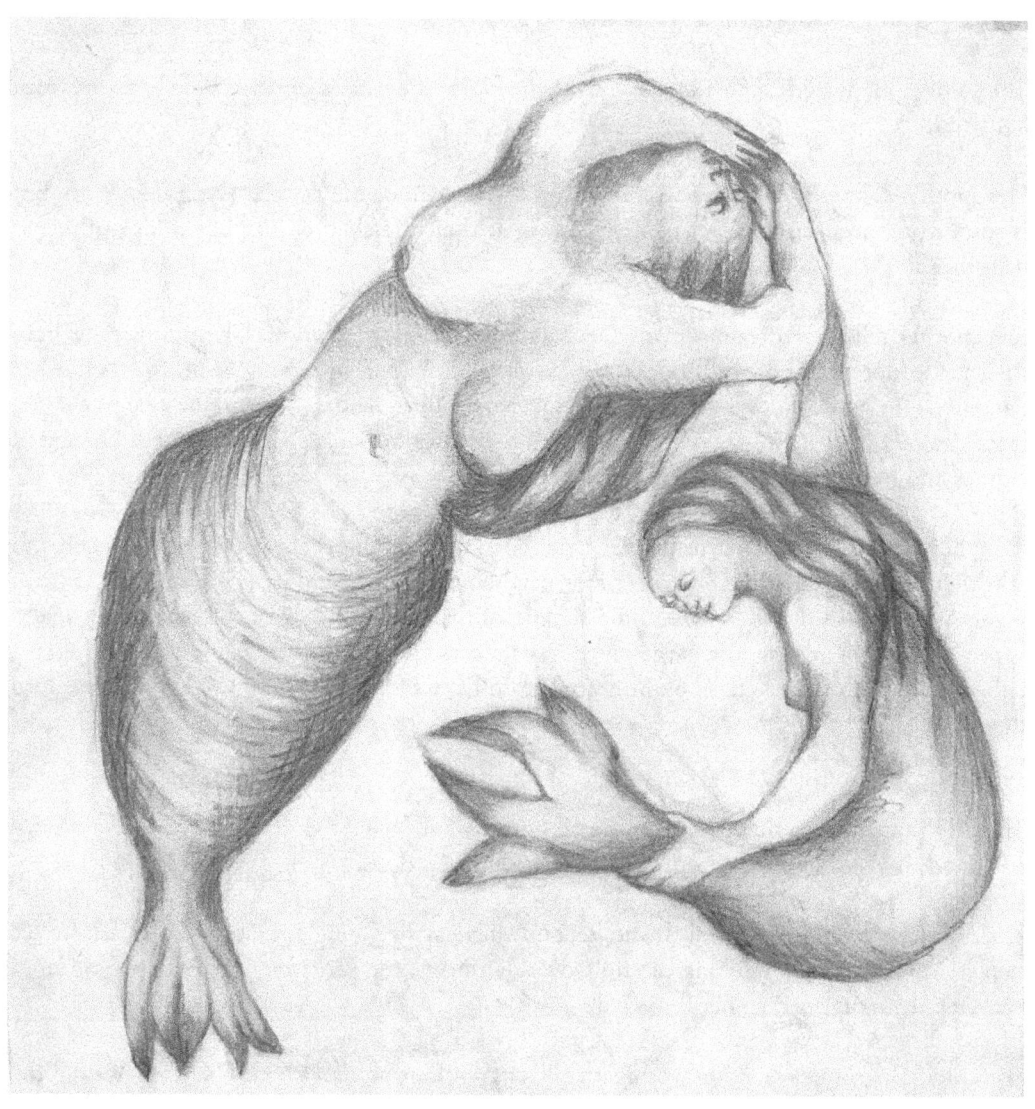

"Mother Daughter Mermaids" by Marla Faith

Deedle Rodriguez-Tomlinson

The *Babaylan*

Somewhere in a barrio of a small town in southern Philippines, a young girl, not quite seventeen, wakes up in a pool of blood. She screams for her mother who runs into her room; she sees what has happened: her daughter has lost her baby.

The young girl, hysterical, insists that during the night, the *manananggal* sucked her baby from her womb.

Her mother asks if she saw the *manananggal*, was aware of the attack. The girl says no, but is sure it had been on their roof; she looks up at their thatched ceiling but finds nothing is disturbed.

Her mother tells her to calm down. *Don't dwell on such things, anak.* She promises to have their next-door neighbors call the town *babaylan* who had been serving as midwife since her daughter found out she was pregnant a little over a month before. She carefully helps the girl from the bed, and leaves the bloody sheets. She bathes her and gives her a fresh change of clothes and has her lie in another room.

Then her mother runs to her next-door neighbors, quickly tells them what has happened and asks that someone fetch the *babaylan*. Her neighbors swear the young girl is telling the truth because they heard the *tik-tik-tik* sound that accompanies the arrival of the *manananggal* and kept vigil that night, hanging garlic on their windows and placing a *buntot pagi* – a stingray's tail – underneath their bed – anything to ward off the monster, in case it tried to come into their home. But they knew – they sensed – the creature could smell the pregnant girl and would go for her.

The neighbors next to them said they heard nothing and suggested that if they heard a *tik-tik-tik* sound, it very likely was simply bats flying over their house.

The *babaylan*, finally arriving at the home, and without the young girl's knowledge, asks to see the bloody bed sheets. Looking carefully over the sheets, the *babaylan* sees it: a little sac amid blood clots no bigger than her fingernail.

She enters the room where the young girl is lying on her mother's bed. She does not tell the young girl what she has found, seeing no need to add to the trauma. She approaches the bed and gently rubs the girl's belly. After saying a prayer under her breath, the *babaylan* takes the girl's hand and tells her that she has indeed suffered a miscarriage.

The young girl wails and the *babaylan* gives her mother herbs with instructions on how to brew a special tea to help the girl relax. She encourages the girl to take it easy as she has experienced a shock to the system. *Get lots of rest and eat nourishing foods*, says the *babaylan*, *like nilagang baka. The iron in the beef will be good for you.*

But the young girl winces, saying food has left a bitter aftertaste in her mouth in the past week. At this, something within the *babaylan* tingles; she shoots the mother a sharp glance. The mother quickly looks away.

By now, news of the girl's loss has spread throughout the barrio and Aling Rosing, the loud *tsismosa* know-it-all from the town proper, has heard what has happened and will declare to anyone who will listen that the mother should have known better than to allow her daughter to have been knocked up by the Manileño who up and fled back to Manila once he heard the girl was pregnant. *Like mother, like daughter,* the town gossip hissed, taking a deep drag from her Marlboro.

The girl's best friend, Lisa, is sobbing quietly in her room. Lisa had been banned by the mother from seeing her daughter because her cousin was the baby's father. It was her cousin who refused to marry the girl because he said he didn't love her. Lisa knew how much her best friend loved her cousin, loved him enough to keep the baby, the way her mother kept her.

The parish priest, believing only in the existence of God the Father, Jesus, Mary, angels and devils, and not in creatures like the *manananggal,* maintains that the mother and her daughter should have come to church more often and prayed for St. Michael's protection, and not have relied on *anting-anting,* worthless amulets peddled by *albularyos* whom he regarded as quack doctors and purveyors of ancient evils.

Back at the young girl's house, the *babaylan* assures her that her baby was not eaten by the *manananggal,* that miscarriages were a common occurrence and that such a loss was not unusual for pregnant women.

But the young girl recounts that the night before, in a dream, she was lying on her bed and could not move. She heard a *tik-tik-tik* sound and suddenly the nipa grass covering the roof of their hut parted and a long slimy tongue slowly reached down to her belly and she was powerless to stop it or move away. In her dream she cried for her mother, but no sound came out – she watched in horror as the *manananggal's* tongue pierced her belly button and sucked out her fetus until, satisfied, it rolled its tongue back up. Through her window, the young girl could see a creature with leathery wings on a detached half body, its entrails hanging, flying into the darkness beyond.

The young girl looks into the *babaylan's* eyes and begs to be believed. She asks the *babaylan* why she felt nothing while she slept; she had heard that a *manananggal's* tongue administers a kind of sedative and painkiller that could drug sleeping victims so that they would not feel the tongue going through the belly and into the womb, sucking out the fetus.

That did give the *babaylan* pause; why had the young girl not felt the cramps and pain that are often associated with a miscarriage?

She looks over at the mother who has busied herself in the girl's room, pulling off the bed sheets and depositing them, as well as the girl's bloodied nightgown and undergarments, into a basket and declaring that she needed to go down to the river to launder everything immediately, asking the *babaylan* if she could please watch over her daughter, that she would not take long. The *babaylan* obliges.

As soon as the mother leaves, the *babaylan* turns to the young girl and persuades her to close her eyes, to try and get some rest. Out of sheer exhaustion and heartbreak, the girl falls asleep.

Quickly, the *babaylan* goes into the kitchen, opening what few cupboards there were. She sees their meager supply of instant noodles, canned sardines, as well as some salt, garlic, ginger -- all things, the *babaylan* thought ruefully, that could supposedly ward off any *aswang*, even a *manananggal*.

She rummages in drawers and looks behind pots and pans but cannot find what she is searching for. Closing her eyes, she uses her acute sense of knowing, her *pakikiramdam*. She takes a deep breath, exhales, then slowly opens her eyes and scans the room. A sack of rice stands by a wall; she feels drawn to it. She walks over, opens the sack, and runs her hand over the grains.

Instinctively, she digs deeper into the sack. She pushes her hand into the rice till her whole arm is immersed in the grains. Soon her hand comes in contact with a plastic bag. She takes hold of it and slowly pulls her hand back up, careful not to spill any grains.

She brings the bag closer to the light from the window; the contents look like potpourri and bits of tree bark – all innocuous-looking but she knew exactly what they were for – aborting a baby.

The *babaylan* guessed that the mother must have obtained it from the *albularyo* that lived deep in the forest, who sold these herbs and roots in secret, as the Church – and subsequently, many lawmakers – frown on any form of contraception, particularly abortion.

She must have made a concoction by boiling the herbs and bark and mixing it in the girl's food, the *babaylan* surmised, which is why the girl complained about food tasting bitter in the past few days; the *babaylan* had heard that the concoction is so bitter that the body can't take it and that helps induce a miscarriage.

And then, in another little plastic bag within the bag, she finds something familiar: valerian root. It can induce a deep sleep but the other reason she is also familiar with it? It is something she prescribes because it helps relieve muscle pain and menstrual cramps.

The *babaylan* sits back in the chair at the little table in the kitchen, stunned.

After a few moments, she slowly gets up and shoves the plastic bag deep into the sack of rice. She closes the sack, and, hearing a small cry coming from the girl's room, returns to tend to her.

The Alley

If she reached out the window, she could almost but not quite touch fingers with the child leaning out the window across the way. She didn't try it, of course. She didn't want him to get silly and fall out. The little boy shouted, "Hello, hello, hello, hello!" As insistent and loud as a parrot. "Hello," she said, and closed the window. Hot. The sky was white and heavy with moisture. She'd arrived yesterday, collapsing into the house as though she'd been washed ashore after a storm. She'd slept beautifully that first afternoon, through hammers and barking dogs and gas-truck loudspeakers, but at night the heat rising up from the cobblestones kept her awake. Or maybe something else caused her to drift through the house in the wine-colored dark.

Her mother was old and confused. The green veins of her withered hands were mountain ranges; her eyes were clouds. Her mother was so confused she thought she'd just had a baby. Once a mother, always a mother? "I don't know what I'm going to do," her mother had said to her. In the memory-care unit, the staff kept life-sized baby dolls for the women to hold, but her mother's baby was in another room, so she said. She whispered that people were outside, having sex in the trees. They were angry because the baby was crying too much. "Maybe I'm too old to raise another one."

"I'll find a good home for it, mom," she promised.

You could be eighty-seven years old and have a baby. It was something to look forward to. No idea of all the wonders that life still had in store. She would keep her promise, keep the baby close, in a little basket in her mind, something warm and comforting to pull out when worries raised their sharp quills.

"Hello, hello!" the child shouted to the empty alley.

Soliloquies: Red and White
Inspired by the Brothers Grimm

The Mother

Remote in a valley, I lived with my two daughters. I'm something of an amateur gardener. Roses are my specialties. And from two bushes, I plucked my girls, one white, one red. Love children, perfectly conceived.

Play can be a protection, better than worry and fear. I sent them alone into the forest. And when they told me of the darkness, the precipice, my heart missed a beat, but I had been there before and so I said, "A beautiful angel in a glittering white dress will watch over you. Do not be afraid."

Snow White

The winter was my time to stay home and play house. That particular winter I scoured the brass kettle so clean that it shone like gold. I lit the fire and hung the kettle over the hearth. Even before he knocked, we readied the house for him. Without an inkling or a clue, without a note or a phone call, we prepared. The fire danced. The shadows flickered. And the kettle shone like gold. Oh, nothing shocks like that we sense is coming when it comes. And on that silent winter night, nothing shocked us quite so much as that bold knock. I hid behind my mother's bed.

To each her own strength. "Quick, Rose Red, it must be a wayfarer in need of shelter," my mother said in answer to my prayer not to be asked. Rose Red unbolted the lock. A big black bear thrust his head through the door. All but our mother trembled.

Rose Red

We learned the charm of peek-a-boo. First he said, "Children, beat my fur a little. It is full of snow." We brought the broom and swept the snow away. We brought a hazel switch and beat the frost away. His growling frightened us. But before long we learned that for him that dark sound was but a harmless stretching and a yawn. He sprawled out before the fire. We grew brave. Tugged at his fur and walked on him. Lifted his eyelid and stared into his eye. He sang his song, "Children, children let me live: Snow White and Rose Red, You'll beat your suitor till he's dead."

The word "suitor" sent us into a pure fit of giggling. Paroxysms of laughter. Which of us would he marry?

The Mother

Time passed. This happened and then that. Summer, autumn, winter, spring. In spring the bear left us. "I must guard my treasure from wicked dwarfs," he said. Snow White grew pensive. In her pocket she kept a bit of his fur. "Mother," she told me, "Under his fur, gold shone through, I think but am not sure."

One brings forth children to give them up to the world, to recapture then for oneself the ways of solitude. I was something of a forester so I sent them to romp in the forest, to gather wood. I was something of a fisher, so I sent them too to splash in a stream, to catch a fish. I was a seamstress and sent them to town to buy needle, thread, laces and ribbon. "Here are two tokens. Catch a trolley," I said. Rose Red took the coins ready to be off, but Snow White lingered in the cottage. She touched each item that she loved. The kettle, the broom, the bleating lamb, the cooing dove, the vase with two roses. "What one of you has, share with the other," I said. "That is all. Hold hands. Now go."

Rose Red

What can I tell you? What I say, I say with the wisdom of hindsight with that particular vision that belongs to an owl. I led the way away holding my sister's hand. We gathered wood. We fished a brook. We rode a trolley. Tangled beards fascinated us. Strange as it may seem, but true. We started to see them everywhere. We found one on a dwarf. We forgot our black furry friend, the bear. Or rather remembered only the mirth of his gruff play. And with the wizened dwarf tried to recapture that perfect childhood memory.

"Nasty toads," he called us. "Blockheads" and "geese." "Silly milk-fed faces." We did not listen. We called him playmate and rescued him, cutting away part of his beard to free him from the cleft of a tree trunk, a knotted fishing line, and the claws of an eagle. "Clumsy clods," he bellowed. "Uncouth brats." What were we to think? A childhood game? Having never heard such words, we did not recognize ingratitude, a shrunken spirit. The soul of our mother loomed so large.

I shudder now to think of it, of what might have been. We came upon the heath on our way back from town. The dwarf again. His long white beard. There on the ground jewels sparkled. Stones glittered in the evening sun. Pearls shone in the rushes. We stood and stared in wonder. The little man danced about. A grasshopper hopping, but turned ashen with rage when he saw us gaping. How close to death, the precipice. Fortunately, the sudden growl of a bear saved all. With one swing of the paw, the dwarf was dead. A spell broken. My sister danced with our black prince. I with his brother.

Snow White

I live with my bear, gold beneath his coat. My sister married his brother. Jewels glitter. We played a game. We found stolen treasure. What one has she shares with the other. That is all. Our present lives, an echo of our romping youth. Our mother? A strong memory. A remote valley. A woman complete in her solitude. A forester walking the forest path. A fisher by the gurgling brook. A seamstress stitching a seam. The polished kettle on the hearth. Needle and thread. Thread and needle. The fire roaring. The shadows on the wall. The bobbin like the seasons turns and turns and turns. Red and white. White and red. A gardener trims two bushes again and then again, plucks two roses for a vase.

Laura Geringer Bass

The Winter Seeds
A Classic Greek Myth Retold

Demeter was so fond of her daughter, Persephone, that she never let the girl out of her sight.

"You don't let her breathe," said her brother King Hades. What would he know about being a mother? He lived in the underworld, lording it over the spirits of the dead. He loved jewels, only jewels.

It was harvest time, and Demeter was busy growing the corn in far away lands. "Please, Mother, may I stay home by myself today? I'm almost grown," begged Persephone. "See, I have my pots of paint. I'll put new stripes on the lilies."

"Just this once," said the goddess, "but take care not to go wandering in the fields." Persephone promised but as soon as her mother's chariot whirled out of sight, she went dancing out into the meadow. Filling her apron with flowers, she noticed an unusual bush covered with blood-red berries.

"I'll pull it up and plant it in Mother's garden to surprise her," she thought. Seizing the shrub, she tugged until, with a loud rumble, the ground cracked asunder. Persephone staggered back, staring into the deep hole she had made in the earth.

A team of black horses snorting smoke tore their way out of the pit, pulling a golden chariot. And in the chariot, sat a man in black armor, wearing a crown.

"Don't be afraid," he said. "I'm your Uncle Hades. Your mother must have told you about me. You'll find me very nice, once we get out of this disagreeable sunshine."

"But I love sunshine!" cried Persephone.

"You'll grow to love me more," he said.

Hades scooped Persephone up in one strong arm, and with the other, whipped the horses until they broke into so swift a gallop they seemed to be flying. "Dry your tears, my little princess," he said. "I'll show you flowers made of diamonds and rubies."

"I'm not your little princess," said Persephone. Then she opened her mouth wide and screamed.

Far, far away, Demeter heard a girl, screaming. The sound troubled her heart. She returned home early to discover that Persephone was gone.

Weeping, Demeter knocked at the door of every cottage, farmhouse, mansion and palace, to ask if anyone had seen her daughter.

At one house, a little gardener's helper pointed a finger at her and laughed loudly. "Do you dare mock a mother in her grief?" cried the goddess, and changed him into a lizard. She might have relented and changed him back, but a hawk spotted the lizard and, swooping down, caught him in its beak and flew away.

Night fell and Demeter lit a torch, stopping her search only long enough to watch it flare. At dawn, she was still searching and the next day and night, and the next. The red flame burned on, never extinguished by rain or wind.

On the seventh day, the goddess saw another torch like her own, gleaming red in the mouth of a cave. On a heap of dry leaves, sat a woman whose dog-shaped head was crowned by a wreath of hissing snakes. It was Hecate, queen of the night.

"Oh, Hecate," cried Demeter. "Tell me for pity's sake, have you seen Persephone?"

"King Hades has taken her to the underworld," said Hecate. "In my opinion, you'll never see her again. Stay here with me and, together, we'll be the two most wretched women in the world."

"No!" cried Demeter. "Persephone is not a pretty gem my brother can pluck for his collection."

"Persephone will drink from the River Lethe and forget about you," said Hecate.

"My daughter will not forget me," said Demeter.

All alone, never resting, never sleeping, holding her undying torch, Demeter continued her search the world over. She suffered so and roamed about so wildly that people ran when they saw her coming. Thwarted, she came to a dreadful decision. Not a stalk of grain or an ear of corn, not a potato or a turnip would grow until her daughter was returned home. Not a single spear of asparagus would dare poke out of the ground. And she forbade the flowers to bloom.

"If the grass is to be green again," she said, "it must grow along the path my daughter walks coming home to me."

Not far from the gates to Hades, was an iron bridge overhung by a giant cypress. The black stream gliding beneath it moved slowly as if it was not sure which way to flow.

"The River Lethe," said Hades, leading the thirsty Persephone along its banks. "One sip of the waters and you will no longer miss your mother."

Persephone shrank back. "I will not drink," she said.

"You've been here for days, Persephone. You're thirsty," said Hades. "You must drink. Take one sip, just one."

"I won't!" cried the girl.

Every night, Persephone woke, sick with hunger and hungry for home.

 Hades presented her with a garden plot all her own where she could, like her mother, make things grow. Surrounded by black orchids, nightshade, henbane and hellebore, Persephone knelt on the damp ground. "Oh mother," she whispered, "where are you?"

"I met your mother once," said a voice. Startled, Persephone rose and saw a spirit boy standing there, staring at her with peculiar lidless eyes.

"She changed me into a lizard," he said. "If I hadn't met her, I wouldn't be here." The boy drew closer. "You're hungry, aren't you? Come with me."

He led her through thick brambles and creepers to a clearing. A single tree stood in a grassy circle.

"Pomegranates!" whispered Persephone. "My favorite."

The fruits were round and red. The boy picked one and brought it to his mouth. "No one will see us," he said. "No one will know." He cracked it open and ate, his mouth smeared red with juice. "Eat," he said, holding it out to her.

Persephone dug out the tiny tart seeds. One. Two. Three. She put them in her mouth and swallowed.

A shout split the air. Hermes, silver-winged messenger of the gods, descended. "The earth is dying," he said. "I've come to take you home."

Home. Persephone had heard that word in her dreams so many times, she thought she was dreaming now.

"King Hades, King Hades!" yelled the lizard boy, rushing off with the half-eaten pomegranate in his hand. "Persephone is flying away!"

Demeter sat on her doorstep, staring at the torch burning in her hand. Lifting her head, she was surprised to see a sudden band of green appear across the parched fields.

"Does the earth disobey me?" she exclaimed. "Is it turning green when I've commanded it to be barren until my daughter is safe in my arms?"

"Then open your arms, Mother," cried a beloved voice.

Persephone came running and flung herself into her mother's arms. Clinging to one another, they wept.

At last, when their hearts had grown quiet, Demeter studied Persephone. "My child," she said, "did you taste the food of the dead while you were in Hades' kingdom?"

"Not one bite," said Persephone, "until today, when I met a strange boy who said you changed him into a lizard."

Her mother turned pale.

"He showed me a pomegranate tree and…Oh, Mother, I know I shouldn't have, but I ate three tiny seeds."

Demeter moaned. "For each seed," she said, "you must spend one month of every year in Hades' underworld. Nine months with me, three with Hades. As long as you are there, nothing shall grow. The earth will mourn with me and those cold months shall be called winter."

Persephone kissed her mother and stroked her hair.

Looking into her daughter's eyes, Demeter saw that Persephone had changed. Before she was kidnapped, she had been a child whose light step on the hillside made it bloom. Now, every spring, she would again make the hillsides bloom but always with the memory of the coming winter when the earth would sleep under frost.

Silently, mother and daughter sat close together, watching the new moon rise over the distant sea. Demeter heard the waves, hissing like the snakes on Hecate's head. "In my opinion, you will never see your daughter again," Hecate had said. But here was Persephone, sitting by her side, alive and more radiant than ever.

The torch Demeter had carried all those days, looking for her lost child, flickered and went out.

Persephone took her mother's hand. "Are you sad because someday soon I will leave you again?" she asked.

"Yes," said Demeter. "And because you are no longer a child."

Persephone smiled, her lips still red from the juice of the pomegranate.

"All that time, when I was away from you," said Persephone, "you were still with me, Mother."

"And you with me," said her mother.

And at long last, she too could smile.

K.W. Oxnard

Drain

He tried to save them: seven hennaed strands of her hair, some as thick as the legs of the flies dying in the kitchen, others as gossamer as her lost eyelashes. All precious, all circling the bathtub drain like kelp in a gyre. The gyre in the Bay of Fundy that, in her last good summer, swallowed those unsuspecting kayakers. The kayakers she'd read about in the *Portland Press Herald* and said, Poor things, they must have been new to the coast. The coast she loved, the glaciated hills of Maine so alien to her flatlander childhood. A childhood, she had explained to him, full of longing for what she could not see, years of willing South Georgia clouds into mountains. Mountains like the ones she insisted on climbing wherever they found themselves, Colorado, Norway, the Philippines. Their Filipino guides laughing in the tent, sharing canteens of fresh coconut water near the crater of the volcano. A volcano called Mayon--Beautiful, like her--which would erupt years later, carving red trenches into black soil under the copra groves. Copra, its husks giving off long, human-like, dark red hairs that clogged the gutters, scaring the town's children. Children they would never have despite freezing her eggs before chemo, saving them for after remission when she could stomach more than coconut water. The water now spilling down the drain, taking her away from him again and again, each hair another loss, another death as it spiraled into a dark red gyre on its journey to the sea.

Kate Gehan

In the Tall Grass the Rabbits Are on the Move

We are on our knees every night praying for your family, the cashier says whenever I pick up a pepperoni pizza. You can spare people what they don't need to know. You can pretend you are not a person in a family where it will never, not ever, be about you again.

No one talks about the outcome, especially my father, who is sidelined by my mother's faith: Nick survived for a reason and will improve and one day return to her. No one says maybe it would have been better if Grandpa had been a sloppier fisherman, less quick to snatch Nick from the water, or if the lifeguard performing the compressions had been less competent. We might be a family in a different kind of perpetual failure.

A pastor who once bought insurance from my father camps out on our yard broadcasting his Bible across social media to thousands of people who suddenly care about us, and no one stops him. Nick didn't die, *Halleluiah*. The nation sends money and private jets to special treatment centers. Salt lamps, essential oils, teddy bears. Prayer circles, food trains, 5K Runs.

*

My mother will later tell me of the nights at 2 am when she snuck out to the field next to the church, which is anchored in one corner by a life-size statue of Mary. They shared the moonlight with the rabbits and my mother came to realize the Virgin is chipped plaster, not marble like she'd believed. She fruitlessly willed the church bells to ring, wore earbuds and spun in circles, The Clash exacerbating her tinnitus. Even while she swam through self-indulgent nostalgia for the time before this mess, she will say she was buoyed by the beautifully absolute understanding that loss is not if but when, *Amen*.

Rochelle Williams

Shoe Boxes

Is this how you found them?

Yes.

You haven't touched anything?

No, I lie.

I had opened the lids of a half-dozen of the boxes and peered inside while he was downstairs. In each box, nestled on a bed of pink satin, a single object: sewing shears; a well-used mesh tea ball; a single ballpoint pen; a tarot card (the magician); an empty, emerald-green leather wallet with dirt in its creases.

I stand in the closet with the police officer, surrounded by the chilling evidence of my mother's madness.

Her body, or what remained of it, had been discovered and removed after a neighbor reported the smell. The bedding and mattress were removed, too. The word, "liquefaction," was on the medical examiner's report.

My mother's body turned to liquid while I was as far away from her as I could possibly get. An indefatigable detective located me, said he found a phone number on a piece of paper under the utensils in a kitchen drawer with the name "Amy" and thought it was worth a try. I had not spoken with my mother in all the years since I not so much left home as escaped it when I was eighteen.

My father died young, I was an only child, as were both my parents, there was no one else for the detective to call.

As a child I loved to hide in here, tucking myself into the folds of her silky dresses, her cool cotton shirts, the scent of Jean Naté dusting powder faintly perfuming the air. Now, immaculate pink shoeboxes printed with tiny white hearts are stacked from floor to ceiling in perfectly even rows. There are no clothes in this closet. No shoes, apparently, in these identical shoeboxes. The clothes rods and shelving, the built-in shoe racks that held high heels studded with rhinestones and elegant satin pumps she ordered from Bergdorf's in her extra-narrow size, have all been removed. It took some arranging, all this tidy, frightening, meaningless, ruthlessly contained chaos.

The officer's radio crackles. I think of my own gruesomely ordered, disposable life—my minimalist wardrobe, my throwaway personal items, my spare, anonymous apartment in a city half-way around the world where no one knows anything about me—and suddenly I feel so sick I have to run for the bathroom. I sit on the edge of the cold pink porcelain tub and sweat, fighting back nausea. When it passes I stand and look in the mirror. My face doesn't look right. I don't recognize myself. I see with a shock that is like a body blow: I haven't escaped her at all.

Melissa Ostrom

Banked for Winter Travel

On the Empire Service Amtrak, I settled in a seat beside a woman whose knitting project already filled her lap and occupied her hands. She didn't smile but greeted me with a measured nod, as if allotting a certain number of stitches to the down and up motions of her head.

She had long since cast her needle. Wooly fabric of mottled browns and greens rippled to her knees in rows of plain stitches and purls. The knitted lines made thousands of vertical arrows, like layers of migrating geese. She sat closest to our window, and whenever my eyes drifted to the passing December morning, raw with severe skies and emptied trees, I couldn't help but keep track of her progress.

With every passing hour, the notebook under my hands didn't have nearly as much to show for itself as the fabric thriving between her fingers. The crossing needles mildly clucked at my still pen. And by the time we began to pull through the Hudson Highland along the clouded river that straightened for a stretch like a determined mouth, her blanket had surged over her legs and half-covered even mine.

She paused once to apologize and tried to gather the folds away.

"Oh, no. I'm fine. It's nice."

And it was the nicest part of that travel, her industry, then me: a quiet coastal farmhouse in banking-up season, the base of my north side properly insulated, snugly shouldered with a pitch-forked wall of warm seaweed.

NONFICTION

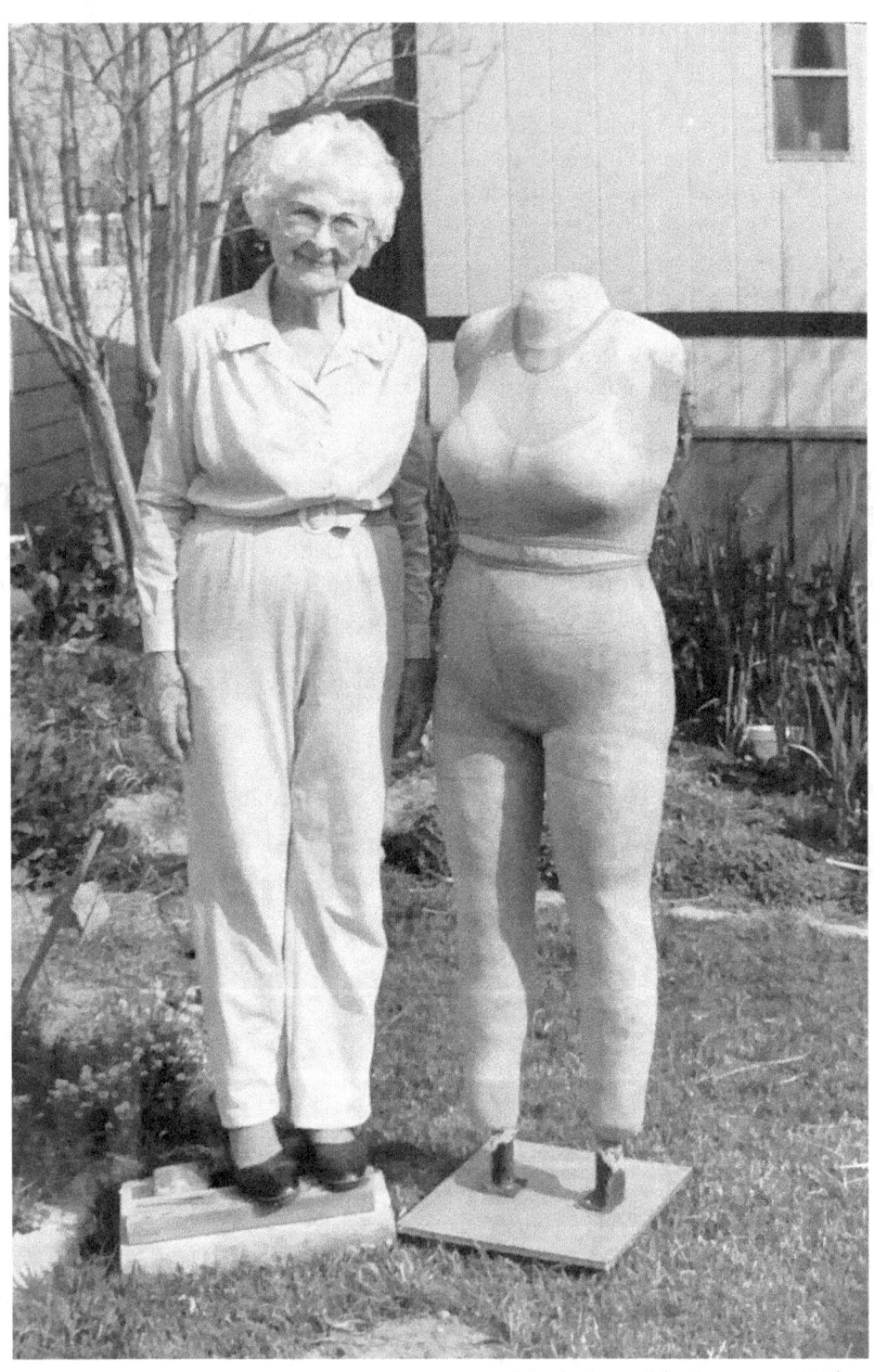

"Body Image" by Lawrence Bridges

Boy Born

We don't make it more than a quarter mile into southern Utah canyon before the Ziploc bag of Swedish fish runs out. It feels like we have traveled a pioneer's road to get to this point, the exhaustion of the summer heat encapsulating us. My oldest son is dogged in his quest for lizards, my middle daughter searching for bones in the shade, and the youngest two, the ones who ate all the Swedish fish with reckless abandon, asking "more, more" before they'd finished what they had in their sandy palms, are sweaty and adorable. One of these two-year old's is mine, she knows the intimacy of me as her mother. And the other two-year old is made up of half my DNA, but he does not know me, not as a mother, or anyone else besides his mother's friend.

This child, the one my friends had tried to conceive for over a decade. Half of me, half of the father of this boy the same size and stature of my daughter. Their small bodies moving through the hot sun, bending in unison to put their hands in the sand beneath the shade of an ancient rock wall.

I would be lying if I said I didn't look at him and wonder if he looks like me. Do his eyes have that peculiar roundness like my own children? Does he walk like me? What is it that I gave to him? If I didn't know his story though, I would never guess I had anything to do with it. In truth, he looks nothing like me.

Still, I wonder weird things like, does he know? Is there something in him that is tethered to me? It doesn't seem that way. I am a shadow here on this desert hike. We are in the same place, the right ages to be a mother and son, but we are not. I am the carrier of snacks, I am the mother of the little girl he walks beside, hardly more. My uterus did not house his body, but his DNA lived inside my ovaries as a microscopic egg for thirty-one years. He comes from one of 22 eggs the doctor extracted the summer I gave myself the fertility shots, had my blood drawn and had an ultrasound every day at noon.

The process to donate my eggs was a brief month-long cycle, a process, a mingling of science, technology and biology, and then there were eight embryos living in a sterile dish, ready to be summoned. For some reason I imagined it would be so much more, more complicated, more time, more pain, but my body obeyed like clockwork, a factory producing what was needed to make this boy. Almost none of his story, or him, beyond those three weeks, is mine at all.

The embryo, unthawed and ready, entered his mother's uterus a year later. I listened over the phone as my friend told me the way they watched the miniature dot, along with the tech who guided it to that point, on the screen next to them. The way it floated through the space of waiting and wondering, and attached itself to the wall, embedded itself—himself, into being. A tiny ship landing on a foreign planet.

I cared for my own two small children when my friend experienced morning sickness and gave herself shots every day to trigger her hormones. I got the call the day he was born and brought dinner over. I held their baby briefly against my own pregnant stomach. Two halves of me multiplied in the moment to make two wholes.

My family, who knows that I donated my eggs to these friends, ask me if I feel attached to this little boy, if I feel something different for him, if it is weird. I do not feel attached to him, I do not feel ownership, but sometimes, when I see him alongside my own children, I do feel a pull to watch him carefully, unsure of what I think I'll figure out.

The summer I filled myself full of hormones and gifted those twenty-two little specs, they distinctly felt not mine. As if I had simply been housing them. I knew I would possibly see the babies produced from them, I knew that one day they would likely know their story was slightly different than other babies. I wish that I could reach into the future and untangle complexity, let them know that they were never mine to begin with, though my DNA is what made them possible. It seems nothing short of a biblical miracle.

We turn to walk back to the car that is parked in a dusty ravine. We go just as slowly as we came. This boy has dark blond curls that are wet with sweat. My daughter's hair is straight as sticks. His shoulders, red with sun are more pale than my daughter's olive complexion. His eyes brown, hers blue. Something must tie them together though. A man walks by us and asks, "Oh! Are they twins?" and I, my husband and little boy's mom all stutter and say something different. I am quick to say no, to relinquish any sense that he might be mine, maybe too adamantly. His mom says, "sort of" without any further explanation, and my husband says, "they're very close in age." All of these things are true, and none of them matter.

Their lives are not un-complex, but it is also a story based in love, which feels very simple. My daughter is smitten by this boy. Later, before bed, we bath them together and after, they twirl in their footy pajamas, while we sit on the couches and laugh at their wildness. They fall to the floor and get up again for nearly an hour. Their small bodies crossing one another, the winding, wild path indistinguishable to parse out.

Kelly Thompson

Yellow Wallpaper

Once, a bird flew into our house, wings a blur, hitting the walls, frantic. "Open the windows!" I yelled. The girls and I chased the bird until it found open air above the kitchen sink. And then we were giddy. In a way, it was like watching myself get sober.

My two daughters rarely saw me drink. When I was in treatment, they attended family program, and were asked to draw a picture of my alcoholism. They both drew a door. I drank behind it.

They were 11 and 13 when I sobered up. The youngest rebelled against my newly sober hypervigilance. I fed, cared for, and clothed my girls but in other ways I'd been missing.

Like the bird who'd flown inside, my daughter wildly banged against the windows I was now determined to keep shut. The open air seemed dangerous.

One night she defied me, escaped. I was furious. Late the next day, I heard knocking. On the other side of the locked screen door stood my girl, the summer evening fading and green behind her.

I didn't open the door. I was prepared and handed her a grocery sack with some clothing and a Big Book of Alcoholics Anonymous on top.

This is not something I'm proud of, though at the time I thought I was being the mother I had needed as a teen. I would provide tough love. I drew a line in the sand. My daughter would not make the same mistakes I had.

All my regret, my own interrupted life, stood between us, the sound of crickets breaking the silence.

The die was cast. Newly recovering, I had a new religion. I'd rebelled against my own fundamentalist upbringing, but conditioning runs deep. Generations of rigidity and my own alcoholic thinking meant my reasoning was faulty. Now I believed I had *the* answer. My daughter's behavior was alcoholic. I was going to save her.

The pendulum swings and mine swung from rebellion to conforming. Seemingly opposites but the same coin. Turn it from front to back, from back to front and it doesn't change. Silver coated, cool; its weight in the hand stays static. Flip it and call heads or tails. One or the other, the price is the same.

My daughter's behavior escalated, and I lost all control. I repeatedly called the police, who did little to nothing to help except take a report. Friends urged me to call anyway, create a "paper trail."

One night she got physical with me when I tried to keep her from leaving, and I called again. The same police officer who'd responded to multiple calls before showed up. He towered above us, shiny badge glinting above the pocket of his blue uniform. He didn't say it, but it was written on his face, "Now what?"

The last time he'd come he'd threatened to take *me* to jail. Surely, I was to blame, the hysterical mother. I stood and faced him, held out my wrists, "Take me."

This time was different. When my daughter cursed in his face, he called social services. She had always acted meek upon his arrival. "Out of control," he said into the phone. Then, though a grown man, it took him five minutes to restrain her.

"Mom, please," she cried. "I'm sorry. I promise." I turned my face. "I can't do this even one more day." I believed my refusal to give in could save her life, where nothing else had gotten through.

My heart hardened. Even as I put on her shoes and tied them, even as my hands were shaking, I believed to let go would be to lose her. I was desperate to control her. She would fight to the end for her right to choose without me.

Handcuffed, she didn't fight me now. I tied double-knotted bows like the ones I made for her when she was four, so the strings wouldn't come untied and trip her.

The police officer, shaken, still angry, escorted her out the door, into the patrol car, and to a shelter for adolescents.

After the door closed, I buried my face against it, and my knees gave way.

What had I done?

It went against everything I believed not to run and stop them. But though all I knew as a mother said to cave, do anything to keep her close, the alcoholic in me knew the game better than the mother. *If you don't say no, if you don't hold this line for her, the same illness that took you down, that killed your grandmother, that wants to destroy you, will take her too.*

A slur on the divine, Marguerite Duras wrote, to describe the shame and stigma projected on alcoholic women, not to mention the alcoholic mother.

My daughter, as I'd feared, found her way into the bottle, into drugs, and away from me just as I fought and found my own way out. In those early sober years, I couldn't see the word-cage made of yellow centered in my mind, how like vines the causes and conditions underlying my drinking wound their way through my mind and body. I did not yet see the wallpaper, nor the walls. I did not see how I'd learned to loathe myself, how I'd ingested a story of original sin. The bottle, as they say, was but a symptom. It took years for my daughter and I to find our way back to each other and into the truth of our original wholeness.

Not only the youngest, but eventually both my daughters found their way into and back out of the bottle, into and back out of what they had drawn as a closed door in their childhood. Some women are born knowing they were meant to fly. The bird who had flown into our home would have beat herself to death against the walls that enclosed her rather than be denied a sky. As would we, I, and my daughters.

Madonna del Latte

To be a virgin but a mother. What is that? *Impossible.*

Not so unlike you, and then me, huddling in the basement to write this, anything—little feet *pat pat pattering* on the ceiling above, demanding in their desire to be heard, held: *witness this*, they say, and I try, but what of writing, what of artistic creation?

(Hear their feet like giant hammers to your head, the wooden floor folding, a century of feet stomping dents into a house where my eldest claims she once saw the ghosts who built these walls.)

The uterus swells and in me grows the third—"The size of a lentil!" I exclaim to the kids as if that's a good thing, this tiny blob that grows from sesame seed to plum in the span of a COVID vaccine schedule.

I'm converting to Judaism but still my childhood in the balcony of St. Theresa's church had me staring at the virgin mother weekly. She was a sculpture muted in sunbeam or fractured in stained glass, and always, *always*, her face of peace and distance, as unapproachable yet intriguing as an unidentifiable mushroom on a forest floor.

"I did it!" a tiny, muted toddler voice cries from beyond the ceiling. What did he do? What did I miss? Write. *Write.* Did I tell you I haven't finished reading Virginia Woolf? Not one book. Not even the one about *a room of one's own.* What is it I crave? That the city around me will empty of every soul, the trees will blossom with cherry fruit, and I'll trample their fallen berries, squish a bloody trail behind me, the haunting silence of a lack of children echoing my victorious laughter as I spill into the dense, leafy embrace of an interminable forest.

In process/disrupted: Three essays, two novels, one short story, and whatever this is—two children who hate brushing their teeth, loathe bath time, want only to run barefoot on the street where syringes are found wrapped to crossbows. Who do I protect first? Child or art? The answer too obvious except sometimes the little one stumbles above and I look up for only a minute before finishing this sentence punctuated by his cries.

The woman whose books I haven't read writes: "One can't write directly about the soul. Looked at, it vanishes; but look at the ceiling, at Grizzle, at the cheaper beasts in the Zoo which are exposed to walkers in Regent's Park, and the soul slips in."

I look up at the ceiling and am stuck again: what can I say about a woman I don't know?

Virgin Mother in medieval paintings, some gilded in gold, framed in light, others painstakingly perfect in their depiction of folds of cherub thighs, angelic cheeks. I want to pinch those cheeks. Cliché. I am nursing three humans—two on the outside, one on the inside—and I struggle to see the angelic here.

Not only virgin, she is also a lactating virgin mother, *Madonna del Latte*, layers of female identity stacked upon one another, images in chapels, adorned to the walls of church halls, in an era when women were banished from these spaces—*virgin lactans*, she's also called, as if her purpose is merely to provide, to sustain the milk and blood of Christ, a form of spiritual nourishment.

In James 19:4-5: "And immediately, the cloud withdrew from the cave and a great light appeared in the cave so that their eyes could not bear it. And a little while later the same light withdrew until an infant appeared. And he came and took the breast of his mother, Mary."

Huddled here still, I read that in Italy, the virgin mother was worshipped in home shrines, even held in pockets, palmed in hands, a tiny figurine of mother and son to rub when praying, when anxious, when bored. Thomas Aquinas, the Italian Dominican friar, believed breastmilk was drawn from uterine blood (the delayed menses of lactation). Is this transubstantiation then, the breastmilk of the virgin becoming the blood of Christ becoming the Eucharist that melted on my tongue at seven years old in St. Theresa's Church, rainbowed mosaic dappling the floor beneath my feet, and I was thinking, "I don't want to eat Jesus," and yet now my toddler claws at me, begs for milk in the middle of a rainy afternoon, in the middle of a quiet night, in the middle of anything about to be something else.

In iconography of the *virgin lactans*, the golden halo framing mother's head and son's, his hand adorning her chest in protection—or ownership? How I pry my son's fingers from twiddling my nipple, how I curse and scorn—*My body!* I affirm protectively and he replies defiantly, *No, mine!*

Madonna del Latte's draping blue robes hide what underneath we women of the gestating tribe know: a swollen vagina, postpartum lochia flowing reddish-brown, staining those same luxurious folds in a constant stream of afterbirth.

What we don't see in her: Aversion. Depleted magnesium so your nipples feel like tiny knives pierce them whenever the toddler latches. Postpartum hemorraging that nearly kills you. Purplish blue stretch marks that never fade. Miasma on your cheeks. Broken tailbones from forceps birth. Third degree tears along the perineum.

Virgin birth: what is that?

Virgin lactation: a pump's rhythmic whir from the "lactation room" in the bowels of an office tower, the blood of Christ *drip drip drip*ping through plastic flange into the hollow basin of a bottle eager to *catch catch catch*, miracle of miracles, the milk of Gods.

Beth Walker

The Anecdote of the Old Woman and the Tiger

Nothing in this world frightens me.
I've roared like a tiger all my life.

> In the famous ninth-century Chinese koan, Zhaozhou comes
> across an old woman minding her business, hoeing trenches
> and rows into a calendar of grief. In the way that only Zen
> monks can never be satisfied, he decides to stop and test her.
>
> What frightens you? he asks. She wipes the sweat, leans on
> her hand-me-down hoe, stares at the unremarkable sky, and
> replies nothing. Nothing does. Then her hoe resumes its
> staccato syntax.
>
> Zhaozhou waits till the old woman's back is turned then
> roars like a lion. Typical of these stories—monks are always
> shouting. But this time the old woman roars back like a tiger.
> The end.

> > That's it? you ask incredulously.
> > That's the end of the story?
> >
> > Never, as is the case with koans.
> >
> > Zhaozhou was famous before the old
> > woman's roar put him in his place, and in the
> > suchness of things, he walked away, still
> > famous. He has continued down the centuries
> > with his good name as his companion while
> > the old woman, well, was just another along
> > the way.
> >
> > The trenches of crossroads are littered with
> > old women, tossed aside from being tested
> > and tested.

But let me tell you more about that hoe and that tiger,
strange stories handed down by calloused hands and scarred hearts
in the thousand years since.

How wood and iron, teeth and bone survive:

Family legend has it that my grandmother's grandmother
whacked her man with a hoe in the fields one thirsty day.

I imagine his head turned like a water wheel and watered
her garden.

What strength that took! What anger! What for?

Did he prowl about the fields, a lion in the twilight,
his eyes glittering and moist?

Did he stalk past the screen door and down
the papered hallway?

Presented with a left or a right, the woman or her girl,
did he pounce on one bed and not the other,
devouring the weakling whole every night?

I can only imagine. Rendered mute, she never wrote her story.

> Ever notice that no one asks why all these
> old women toil alone at these crossroads?
>
> Or why their stories tell about their blood
> trickling down the trenches of their days?
>
> Or why someone's absence from the tale
> is the reason for the telling?
>
> This emptiness is inexpressible, a sky dancer
> without a sky, a bell without a tongue.

And so the story continues:

> When I was a girl I slept with a toy bell tied to my doorknob,
> my baton tucked in the slat of my bed, just in reach.
>
> A half-dozen stuffed bears, cats, and bunnies lay across
> my bony body, sacrifice for a lion who roamed forever
> hungry under a painted sky that never knew the sun.
>
> Every night that bell tinkled so softly it sounded as if even
> the fireflies and the stars were trying not to tremble.
>
> Then I could feel his breath hot and seething, his muzzle
> rooting very moist among the carcasses, while I pretended
> to dream:

In that dream, a little girl
gets gobbled whole.

Awakened by her screams,
her grandmother chops the
lion's head and pries the dead
but still greedy jaws like a
wheezy accordion to play her
granddaughter a lullaby.

"Come out," she sings, "and I
will sew you a fur cloak that
will make you invincible to pain.

Come out, and I will make
you scarlet gloves tipped with
razors. With everything you
touch, you will leave your
mark."

The little girl at last pokes out
her head.

But instead of singing,
she roars and she roars.

That's why nothing in this world frightens me.

I've been a tiger all my life.

"Reflection 1" by Virginia Petrucci

CONTRIBUTORS' NOTES

As a practicing midwife, **Ingrid Andersson** feels privileged to work daily within a world of heroic Mother Figures. Her poetry has been nominated for a Pushcart Prize and Best of the Net and has appeared in *Eastern Iowa Review* (Editor's Choice award), *Midwest Review, Intima: A Journal of Narrative Medicine, Minerva Rising* and other venues. Her debut collection of poetry, *Jordemoder: Poems of a Midwife*, is scheduled for publication by Holy Cow! Press in May 2022.

Cynthia Atkins is the author of *Psyche's Weathers, In The Event of Full Disclosure* (CW Books), *Still-Life With God* (Saint Julian Press 2020). Her work has appeared in numerous journals, including *Alaska Quarterly Review, BOMB, Cleaver Magazine, Diode, Florida Review, Green Mountains Review, Rust + Moth, North American Review, Seneca Review, Tinderbox,* and *Verse Daily*. She is an Interviews Editor for *American Microreviews and Interviews,* and lives in Rockbridge County, VA. www.cynthiaatkins.com.

Laura Geringer Bass is the author of *The Girl With More Than One Heart* (Abrams 2018) a novel about grief and loss that inspired her "life-changing" workshop, "Finding the Heart of Your Story." A mentor at Stonybrook, Southampton as well as Girls Write Now, she serves on the Advisory Board of First Book, an award-winning non-profit organization that has delivered over 200 million books to children in need. Read more about her books at www.laurageringerbass.com.

Francesca Bell is the author of *Bright Stain* (Red Hen Press, 2019), finalist for the Julie Suk Award and the Washington State Book Award, and *What Small Sound* (Red Hen Press, 2023). She translated Max Sessner's collection *Kitchens and Trains* (Red Hen Press, 2023). Her poems and translations appear in journals such as *New Ohio Review, North American Review, Mid-American Review, Prairie Schooner,* and *Rattle*. She lives with her family in Novato, California.

Pam Bernard, poet, memoirist, teacher, and editor, received her MFA from the Graduate Program for Writers at Warren Wilson College, and BA from Harvard University. Her awards include a National Endowment for the Arts Fellowship in Poetry. She has published three full-length collections of poetry, and a verse novel entitled *Esther*, published by CavanKerry Press. She lives in Walpole, New Hampshire and teaches writing at Keene State University.

Rosaleen Bertolino was born in San Francisco and now lives in Mexico. Her stories have recently been published in *New England Review, Bellevue Literary Review, failbetter, Orca,* and *Litro*. Her debut collection, *The Paper Demon & Other Stories,* winner of the 2019 Many Voices Project Prize for Prose, was released by New Rivers Press in December, 2021.

Karen Boissonneault-Gauthier is an Indigenous visual artist, writer and photographer. Most recently she's been a cover artist for *Arachne Press, Pretty Owl Poetry, Wild Musette, Existere Journal, Vine Leaves Literary Journal, Gigantic Sequins, Ottawa Arts Journal* and more. When she's not walking her husky named Kiowa, she's using her visual artwork designing with Art of Where. See www.kcbgphoto.com to see all the places Karen is published.

Cheryl Boyce-Taylor is a poet, and founder of The Calypso Muse Reading Series. The author of five collections of poetry, she was a finalist for the 2018 Paterson Poetry Prize. Her latest book, titled *Mama Phife Represents,* is a verse memoir honoring her son Hip-Hop legend Phife Dawg of the politically conscious band A Tribe Called Quest. Boyce-Taylor,'s new collection, *We Are Not Wearing Helmets,* will be published by Northwestern University Press in Spring 2022.

Lawrence Bridges is best known for work in the film and literary world. His poetry has appeared in *The New Yorker, Poetry,* and *The Tampa Review*. He has published three volumes of poetry: *Horses on Drums, Flip Days,* and *Brownwood*. As a filmmaker, he created a series of literary documentaries for the NEA's "Big Read" initiative, which include profiles of Ray Bradbury, Amy Tan, Tobias Wolff, and Cynthia Ozick.

Cathleen Calbert's writing has appeared in *Ms., The Nation, The New York Times, The Paris Review, Poetry,* and elsewhere. She is the author of four books of poems: *Lessons in Space, Bad Judgment, Sleeping with a Famous Poet,* and *The Afflicted Girls.* Her awards include the 92nd Street Y Discovery Poetry Prize, a Pushcart Prize, the Sheila Motton Book Prize, and the Mary Tucker Thorp Professorship at Rhode Island College.

Patricia Callan is a writer, artist, and educator living in Beverly, MA with husband, daughters, and a teeny-tiny beagle. Her work can be found at *Hawaii Pacific Review, Unstamatic, Adanna Literary Journal* and elsewhere.

Tina Carlson is a NM poet. Her work has appeared or is forthcoming in *Psaltery and Lyre, Cutthroat Journal,* and *Hunger Mountain. Ground, Wind, This Body* (University of New Mexico Press, 2017) was her first book. Her second book, *We Are Meant To Carry Water* (3: A Taos Press) is a collaborative book with two other NM poets and won first place in the 2021 AZ/NM Book Award for Poetry Anthology.

Marina Carreira (she/her/hers) is a queer Luso-American poet artist from Newark, NJ. She is the author of *tantotanto* (Cavankerry Press, forthcoming 2022), *Save the Bathwater* (Get Fresh Books, 2018) and *I Sing to That Bird Knowing It Won't Sing Back* (Finishing Line Press, 2017). She has exhibited her art at Morris Museum, ArtFront Galleries, West Orange Arts Council, Monmouth University Center for the Arts, among others.

Patricia Caspers lives in the foothills of California and is the founding editor of *West Trestle Review.* Her second full-length collection, *Some Flawed Magic,* is now available from Kelsay Press.

Joanne M. Clarkson's fifth poetry collection, *The Fates,* won the Bright Hill Press annual contest and was published in 2017. Her poems have been published in such journals as *Nimrod, American Journal of Nursing, Alaska Quarterly Review, Poetry Northwest,* and *Western Humanities Review.* Clarkson has received an Artist Trust Grant and an NEH grant to teach poetry in rural libraries. A registered nurse, she has specialized in home health and Hospice work. See more at www.JoanneClarkson.com.

Shutta Crum's poems appear in *Blue Mountain Review, Stoneboat, Orchards Poetry Journal, Better Than Starbucks, Nostos, Southern Poetry Review, Beyond Words, Pink Panther, Main Street Rag,* and *Third Wednesday.* Her chapbook *When You Get Here* (Kelsay Books) won a gold Royal Palm Literary Award. She was nominated in 2020 for a Pushcart by *Typehouse.* She is also a children's book author with books on many state reading lists and reviewed by the NY Times. www.shutta.com.

Julie Cyr has been published by *Slipstream, Broad River Review,* and Lost Horse Press in the *Nasty Women Poets Anthology,* among others. She was awarded 2014 Best of Poetry by *Blood and Thunder Journal,* a finalist in the 2016 Rash Awards for Poetry, nominated for a 2019 Pushcart Prize, and won first place in the 2020 Poetry Society of NH Members Contest. Julie holds an MFA in creative writing from Lesley University in Cambridge, MA.

Iris Jamahl Dunkle is an award-winning literary biographer, essayist, and poet. Her work challenges the Western myth of progress by examining the devastating impact that agriculture and over-population have had on the North American West. Taking an ecofeminist bent, her writing challenges the American West's male-oriented recorded history by researching the lives of women. She obtained her MFA in poetry from New York University, and her PhD in American Literature from Case Western Reserve University. Her most recent book is *West : Fire : Archive* (2021).

Jo Angela Edwins has published poems in various venues including *Calyx, New South, descant, Thimble,* and *Adanna.* Her chapbook *Play* was published in 2016. She has received awards from Winning Writers, Poetry Super Highway, and the SC Academy of Authors and is a Pushcart Prize, Forward Prize, and Bettering American Poetry nominee. She lives in Florence, SC, where she serves as poet laureate of the Pee Dee region of South Carolina.

Marla Faith, artist, poet, art educator, lives in Nashville TN. Her art uses personal symbolism to create unique intuitive narratives. Marla has a BFA from the School of the Art Institute of Chicago, and an MS (museum leadership) from Bank Street College in NYC. She is the proud mother of artist Nila (nilafaith.com) Frederiksen. This artwork is about the artist and her daughter. Please view Marla's abundance of joyous, colorful, spiritual art at marlafaith.com

Chelsea Fanning is a writer, poet, editor, feminist, witch from New Jersey. She has an MFA from Drew University and is the poetry editor at *Fatal Flaw Magazine*. Previous work has appeared in *From Whispers to Roars, OyeDrum, Flora Fiction, Literary North,* and *Cauldron Anthology*. Her poetry delves into themes of redefinition, reclamation, wholeness, muchness, womanhood, religion, identity, gender, rebirth, and regeneration.

Beatriz F. Fernandez is the author of *The Ocean Between Us* (Backbone Press, 2017) and *Shining from a Different Firmament* (Finishing Line Press, 2015) which she presented at the Miami Book Fair International. She has read her poetry on South Florida's NPR news station and is a former grand prize winner of the Writer's Digest Poetry Award. She has been nominated for the Pushcart prize three times in the last seven years. Tweet her @nebula61.

Katherine Gaffney completed her MFA at the University of Illinois at Urbana-Champaign and is currently working on her PhD at the University of Southern Mississippi. Her work has previously appeared or is forthcoming in *jubilat, Harpur Palate, Mississippi Review, Meridian,* and elsewhere. Her first chapbook, *Once Read as Ruin,* was recently published by Finishing Line Press.

Michelle Gallagher is originally from Ireland, now residing in Germany. She graduated with a BA in Fine Art from Limerick, Ireland (LSAD) in 2002. Specializing in a multidisciplinary practice ranging from photography to ceramics. Gallagher worked as an art educator and artist initially in Ireland, Botswana and Hungary before settling in Germany. She has participated in a variety of group shows both online and offline. She is a member of Scottish based Spilt Milk Gallery. The representation of gender in a cultural context, specifically the female gender and the feminine, inspiration comes from observations in everyday life and the family and society at large. With an art practice is firmly rooted in the processes of making, the materials used dictate and guide the work directly, Gallagher views the materials as a partner in the realization of the idea, a collaboration.

Kate Gehan's debut short story collection, *The Girl and The Fox Pirate,* was published by Mojave River Press in 2018. Her writing has appeared in *SmokeLong Quarterly, McSweeny's Internet Tendency, Split Lip Magazine, People Holding, Literary Mama,* and *Cheap Pop,* among others. She is nonfiction editor at *Pithead Chapel.* Find her work at kategehan.com.

Joyce Goldenstern lives in Chicago and writes fiction often inspired by folktales. Her novel *In Their Ruin* will by published by Black Heron Press in 2023.

Tzivia Gover is the author of *The Mindful Way to a Good Night's Sleep* (Storey Publishing), *Joy in Every Moment* (Storey Publishing) and *Learning in Mrs. Towne's House* (Levellers Press). Her work has appeared in *Poets & Writers, Lilith, The New York Times,* and dozens of periodicals and anthologies. She combines dreamwork and writing in Dreaming on the Page workshops online and in person. She received her MFA in writing from Columbia University. Visit www.tziviagover.com.

Abby Templeton Greene is the author of three books of poetry: *A Blue House to Sleep In,* forthcoming with Finishing Line Press, *Prayer from a Magdalena Jail Cell* and *An Avocado Slowly Falling,* a book of bilingual poems written in English and Spanish. Her work has been published in *McSweeneys, Calyx Journal, RATTLE, Pilgrimage, The Wazee* and other journals. Visit her at abbytempletongreene.com.

Lara Henneman writes fiction, essays, and poetry. Her work is featured in *Sky Island Journal, McSweeney,'s Internet Tendency, Mutha Magazine, Scary Mommy* and more. She is currently working on her first novel. She has a BA from Brown University and an MA from the University of Denver School of International Studies. She lives in Maryland with her growing family. Find her on Twitter @lhenpen or join her reader list at www.larahenneman.com.

Rebekah Denison Hewitt's work has appeared, or is forthcoming in *Poetry Northwest, The Rumpus,* and *Narrative.* She is an assistant poetry editor at Orison Books. She lives in Wisconsin with her husband and four children and works as a librarian.

Ashley Mae Hoiland has published two books of creative non-fiction. She currently lives in Utah with her three children and husband. She teaches online writing courses at minetotell.com.

Carolina Hospital's poetry collections include *Key West Nights and Other Aftershocks* (Anhinga Press), The *Child of Exile* (Arte Publico Press), and *Myth America*, a collaboration with Maureen Seaton, Holly Iglesias and Nicole Hospital-Medina, (Anhinga Press). She has edited two anthologies of Cuban American literature and her work has appeared in national publications, such as the *Norton Anthology of Latino Literature* and Bedford/St. Martin's *Florida Literature*. She lives between Miami and Palm Coast, Florida.

Originally from Chisinau, Moldova, **Romana Iorga** lives in Switzerland. She is the author of two poetry collections in Romanian. Her work in English has appeared or is forthcoming in various journals, including *New England Review, Gulf Coast, Salamander*, as well as on her poetry blog at clayandbranches.com.

Jen Karetnick's fourth full-length book is *The Burning Where Breath Used to Be* (David Robert Books, September 2020), an Eric Hoffer Poetry Category Finalist and a Kops-Fetherling Honorable Mention. Karetnick has won the Tiferet Writing Contest for Poetry, Hart Crane Memorial Prize, and Anna Davidson Rosenberg Prize, among others. Co-founder and managing editor of *SWWIM Every Day*, she has work appearing recently in *Barrow Street, The Comstock Review, december, Terrain.org*, and elsewhere. See jkaretnick.com.

Sarah Key's work includes cookbooks, non-fiction work on *Huffington Post* and *HeartWood Literary Magazine*, and dozens of published poems. Her work has appeared in anthologies like N*asty Women Poets* and literary journals such as *The Georgia Review, Calyx, Poet Lore*, and *Tuesday; An Art Project*. From the Frost Place to Cave Canem, Sarah has studied poetry and now learns from her students at a community college in the South Bronx where they call her Poet-in-Practice.

Merie Kirby grew up in California. She lives in Grand Forks, ND and teaches at the University of North Dakota. She is the author of *The Dog Runs On* (Finishing Line Press, 2014) and *The Thumbelina Poems* (Red Bird Chapbooks, 2015). Her poems have been published in *Quartet Journal, Midwest Poetry Review, Avocet,* and other journals; she also writes operas and art songs in collaboration with composers.

Elizabeth Lara's poems have appeared in numerous anthologies and journals, both in print and online. She co-edited *Happiness: The Delight-Tree, An Anthology of Contemporary International Poetry*, and curated the MER Online folio "Soy Mujer: Latinx Poets of the Diaspora." Her bilingual chapbook, *Fire in the Mind / Fuego en la Mente*, was published in 2019.

B. Tyler Lee is the author of one poetry collection, *With Our Lungs in Our Hands* (Redbird Chapbooks, 2016), and her essay "A Large Volume Of Small Nonsenses" won the 2020 Talking Writing Contest. Her work has appeared or is forthcoming in *32 Poems, Crab Orchard Review, Hayden's Ferry Review, Blue Mesa Review, Qwerty, The Hunger, Dream of the River: LGBTQ+ Anthology* (Jacar Press), and elsewhere. She teaches in the Midwest.

Julia Lisella's books include *Always* (WordTech Editions, 2014), *Terrain* (WordTech Editions, 2007), and a chapbook, *Love Song Hiroshima* (Finishing Line Press, 2004). Her poems are widely anthologized, and are forthcoming or appear in *Pangyrus, Lily Poetry Review, Ploughshares, Paterson Literary Review, Mom Egg Review, Nimrod, Exit 7, Ocean State Review* and others. She is a professor of English at Regis College, and co-curates the Italian American Writers Association (IAWA) Reading Series in Boston. Her collection, *Our Lively Kingdom*, finalist for the Lauria/Frasca Prize, will be published by Bordighera Press in the fall of 2022.

Poet, writer, **Tamara J. Madison**, is the author of *Threed, This Road Not Damascus; Kentucky Curdled*, and *Sistuh's Sermon on the Mount* (poetry), and *Collard County* (fiction). She is the creator and host of "BREAKDOWN: The Poet & The Poems," a YouTube poetry conversation series that features poets and their poetry as inspiration for everyday life. She is a fellow of Anaphora Arts Writing Residency with an MFA from New England College. Visit www.tamarajmadison.com.

Shikha Malaviya is an Asian-American poet & writer. She is co-founder of The (Great) Indian Poetry Collective, a mentorship model press. Her poems have been nominated for the Pushcart Prize and featured in *PLUME, Prairie Schooner* and other fine publications. Shikha has been a featured TEDx speaker and was selected as Poet Laureate of San Ramon, California. She is an AWP poetry mentor and Mosaic America Fellow. Her book of poems is Geography of Tongues.

Katie Manning is the founding editor-in-chief of *Whale Road Review* and a professor of writing at Point Loma Nazarene University in San Diego. She is the author of *Tasty Other*, which won the 2016 Main Street Rag Poetry Book Award, and her fifth chapbook, *28,065 Nights*, is available from River Glass Books. Her poems have appeared in *december, The Lascaux Review, New Letters, Poet Lore*, and many other venues. Find her online at www.katiemanningpoet.com.

Libby Maxey is a senior editor at *Literary Mama*, where she has been on staff since 2012. Her poems have appeared in *Emrys, THINK, The Maynard, Stoneboat, Crannóg* and elsewhere, and her first poetry collection, *Kairos* (2019), won Finishing Line Press's New Women's Voices Chapbook Competition. Her nonliterary activities include singing classical repertoire, mothering two sons, and enjoying the woods of Western Massachusetts.

Colleen Michaels's poems have appeared in journals and anthologies including *Passages North, Cider Press Review, Barrelhouse,* and *Raising Lilly Ledbetter: Women Poets Occupy the Work Space*. Her poems have been commissioned as installations for The Massachusetts Poetry Festival. She directs the Writing Studio at Montserrat College of Art (Beverly, Massachusetts), and hosts the Improbable Places Poetry Tour, bringing poetry to unlikely places like tattoo parlors, laundromats, and swimming pools. Yes, in the swimming pool.

MaryAnn L. Miller the author of *Falling into the Diaspora* forthcoming from Finishing Line Press in 2023, *Cures for Hysteria* (FLP 2018) and *Locus Mentis* (PS Books 2012.) has been thrice nominated for a Pushcart Prize. Her work has appeared in *Wild River Review, Presence Journal, Ovanque Siamo, Passager, International Review of African America Art,* and the anthologies *Illness as a Form of Existence,* and *Welcome to the Resistance*. She has Hyperkalemic Periodic Paralysis.

Matthew Murrey's poems have appeared widely, recently in *Okay Donkey, 2River View*, and *Red Headed Stepchild*. He is an NEA Fellowship recipient, and his collection, *Bulletproof*, was published in 2019 by Jacar Press. He is a public school librarian in Urbana, Illinois. He and his partner have two grown sons. His website is at https://www.matthewmurrey.net/ and he's on Twitter @mytwords.

Melissa Ostrom is the author of *The Beloved Wild* (Feiwel & Friends, 2018), a Junior Library Guild book and an Amelia Bloomer Award selection, and *Unleaving* (Feiwel & Friends, 2019). Her short stories have appeared in many journals and been selected for *Best Small Fictions 2019, Best Microfiction 2020, Best Small Fictions 2021,* and *Best Microfiction 2021*. She teaches English at Genesee Community College and lives with her husband and children in Holley, New York.

K. W. Oxnard's fiction has appeared in *Story, Columbia Journal, Madison Review, Reed* and *Tahoma Literary Review*. A graduate of New York University's, MFA program in fiction, she was one of two fiction winners in the 2021 *december* Magazine Curt Johnson Prose Awards. After years of teaching writing at the college level, in 2004 she moved back to her hometown of Savannah, Georgia, where she lives and writes surrounded by Spanish moss and childhood memories.

Theta Pavis is a writer living in Jersey City. Her poetry has appeared in *Spillwords, the Journal of New Jersey Poets, The Red Wheelbarrow* and *Mom Egg Review*. Her journalism has been published in *Wired* and *Medium*. She is the Director of Student Media at New Jersey City University and was recently named Journalism Educator of the Year by the New Jersey chapter of the Society of Professional Journalists.

Toni Pepe is chair and assistant professor of photography at Boston University. Her photographs and installation work explore the construction of identity, specifically the icon of the mother. Pepe was a finalist for the Massachusetts Cultural Council Fellowship, a Critical Mass top 50, a Review Santa Fe 100, and was most recently awarded an Artist Trust Grant. Her work is in the permanent collections at the Danforth Art Museum, the Magenta Foundation, and private collections.

Virginia Petrucci is a writer, artist, and law student, and the author of two poetry chapbooks: *The Salt and the Song* and *Recipes and How To's*. Her writing has previously appeared in *Mom Egg Review* as well as *Terrain, The Gay and Lesbian Review,* and *Best New Writing*, among others. She has been nominated for the Pushcart Prize and Best American Short Stories. She lives in California with her two children.

Susan Rich is an award-winning poet, editor and essayist. She is the author of *Gallery of Postcards and Maps: New and Selected Poems, Cloud Pharmacy, The Alchemist's Kitchen, Cures Include Travel* and *The Cartographer's Tongue /Poems of the World*. She has received awards from Artists Trust, PEN USA, Times Literary Supplement, and the Fulbright Foundation. *Blue Atlas* is forthcoming from Red Hen Press in 2024. You can visit her at www.poetsusanrich.com

Susanna Rich is an Emmy Award nominee, Fulbright Fellow, and founding producer of Wild Nights Productions, LLC. She is the author of five poetry collections, most recently *Surfing for Jesus* and *SHOUT! Poetry for Suffrage*. She wrote, composed, and recorded the musical, "Shakespeare's *itches: The Women v. Will." Visit at www.wildnightsproductions.com.

Deedle Rodriguez-Tomlinson was born and raised in the Philippines. Her essay on her experience during Covid-19 lockdown was published in the 2020 Australasian Association of Writing Programs special issue *TEXT: The In/completeness of Human Experience*. Her poems have appeared in the literary issue of *Silliman University Journal*, and *Tomas*, UST literary journal, both in the Philippines. One of her poems is also included in *Under The Storm: An Anthology of Contemporary Philippine Poetry*.

Leah Sandals is a writer and editor based in Toronto. Her poetry and short fiction have also been published in *Prism International, Room Magazine* and *Freefall*.

Anne Owen Shea grew up in Rochester, Minnesota, where she lives with her husband Brendan and four-year-old son Harry. She received a M.A in English from Iowa State University and an M.F.A in Creative Writing from University of Illinois, Urbana-Champaign. Her work has appeared in *Indiana Review, Memoir Magazine, Blue Earth Review* and it is forthcoming in *Cimarron Review*. Anne teaches college-level Reading and English courses.

Zoe Smith-Holladay is a 17-year-old creative writing major at the Denver School of the Arts. When she is not writing poetry, she is playing with her dog, sewing or designing a new fashion piece, or daydreaming about rowing somewhere beautiful.

RaShell R. Smith-Spears is an associate professor of English at Jackson State University in Jackson, MS, where she teaches creative writing and literature. She has published poetry and short fiction in several journals and anthologies including *Gumbo Magazine, Sycorax's Daughters, Mississippi Noir, Dying Dahlia Review,* and *Black Magnolias Literary Journal*.

Kaitlin Solimine is the author of *Empire of Glass* (Ig Publishing, 2017), which was a finalist for the Center for Fiction First Novel Prize and the CLMP Firecracker Awards. Her writing has been published in *The Guardian, Guernica Magazine, LitHub, National Geographic, The Wall Street Journal*, and more. She is the recipient of several literary residencies and scholarships and a columnist for *Motherscope*. She resides in San Francisco with her partner and two children.

Natalie Solmer is founder and editor-in-chief of *The Indianapolis Review* and an Assistant Professor of English at Ivy Tech Community College. A mother to two sons, she's also a former florist who sometimes creates visual art and visual poems. Her poetry and art can be found in such places as: *Colorado Review, Pleiades, EcoTheo Review, The Babel Tower Notice Board*, and *Yes, Poetry*.

Judith Sornberger's full-length poetry collections are: *Angel Chimes: Poems of Advent and Christmas* (Shanti Arts, 2020), *I Call to You from Time* (Wipf & Stock, 2019), *Practicing the World* (CavanKerry, 2018) and *Open Heart* (Calyx Books). Her prose memoir *The Accidental Pilgrim: Finding God and His Mother in Tuscany* is from Shanti Arts. She is professor emerita of Mansfield University where she taught English and Women's Studies. She can be found at www.judithsornberger.net.

Margo Taft Stever's collections include *Cracked Piano* (CavanKerry Press, 2019); *Ghost Moose* (Kattywompus Press, 2019); *The Lunatic Ball* (2015); *The Hudson Line* (2012); *Frozen Spring* (2002) and *Reading the Night Sky* (1996). Her poems have appeared widely in Verse Daily, Plume, Prairie Schooner, Connecticut Review, upstreet, and *Salamander*. She is founder of the Hudson Valley Writers Center and founding and current co-editor of Slapering Hol Press. She lives in Sleepy Hollow, New York (www.margotaftstever.com).

Richard Stimac writes poetry about growing up in the Rustbelt. Richard published poetry in *Faultline, Havik* (2021 Best in Show for Poetry), *Michigan Quarterly Review, Penumbra, Salmon Creek Journal, Wraparound South,* and others, and an article on Willa Cather in *The Midwest Quarterly.*

Alison Stone has published seven full-length collections, *Zombies at the Disco* (Jacar Press, 2020), *Caught in the Myth* (NYQ Books, 2019), *Dazzle* (Jacar Press, 2017), *Masterplan,* collaborative poems with Eric Greinke (Presa Press, 2018), *Ordinary Magic,* (NYQ Books, 2016), *Dangerous Enough* (Presa Press 2014), and *They Sing at Midnight,* which won the 2003 Many Mountains Moving Poetry Award. She has been awarded *Poetry's* Frederick Bock Prize and *New York Quarterly's* Madeline Sadin Award. www.stonepoetry.org www.stonetarot.com

Melissa Studdard's poetry collections include *I Ate the Cosmos for Breakfast, Like a Bird with a Thousand Wings* (chapbook), and *Dear Selection Committee* (forthcoming May 2022). Her work has been featured by PBS, NPR, *The New York Times, The Guardian,* and more. Her awards include the Lucille Medwick Award from the Poetry Society of America, The *Penn Review* Poetry Prize, and the Tom Howard Prize for Winning Writers. www.melissastuddard.com.

Elizabeth Sylvia (she/her) is a writer of poems and other lists who lives with her family in Massachusetts, where she teaches high school English and coaches debate. Elizabeth,'s work is upcoming or has recently appeared in *Salamander, Slipstream, Crab Creek, Pleiades,* and a bunch of other wonderful journals. She is currently working on a verse investigation of the writer Elizabeth Barstow Stoddard. esylviapoetry@gmail.com.

L.J. Sysko's work has appeared/is forthcoming in *The Missouri Review's* "Poem a Week," *Mississippi Review, Ploughshares, Best New Poets, Radar,* and her poetry chapbook: *Battledore* (Finishing Line Press, 2017), among others. A 2022 Palm Beach Poetry Festival Thomas Lux Scholar, Sysko has been honored with both Virginia Center for Creative Arts and Delaware Division of the Arts Fellowships as well as finalist recognition from *Copper Nickel's* Jake Adam York Prize, *Marsh Hawk Press,* and *The Missouri Review's* Jeffrey E. Smith Editors' Prize, among others. You can learn more about her online at ljsysko.com.

Kailey Tedesco is the author of *She Used to be on a Milk Carton, Lizzie, Speak,* and *FOREVERHAUS* (April Gloaming Publishing & White Stag Publishing). She is a senior editor for *Luna Luna Magazine,* and she teaches a course on the archetype of the witch in literature at Moravian University. You can find her work featured in *Gigantic Sequins, Fairy Tale Review, Black Warrior Review, Passages North* and more. For further information, please visit kaileytedesco.com.

Dawn Terpstra lives in Iowa where she leads a communications team. Her poetry appears in current and forthcoming publications, *Main Street Rag, Midwest Review, The Night Heron Barks, Briar Cliff Review, Citron Review, San Pedro River Review, SWWIM, Third Wednesday,* and *Eastern Iowa Review.* Her work was selected as Honorable Mention in the *Midwest Review's* 2021 Great Midwest Poetry Contest. Her chapbook, *Songs from the Summer Kitchen,* is forthcoming in September from Finishing Line Press.

Kelly Thompson has been published in *BOMB, LARB, VIDA Review, Guernica, Brevity, Yoga Journal, Electric Literature, Entropy, Oh Comely, Proximity, Manifest Station* and other literary journals and has been nominated for two Pushcarts, most recently for "Monsters I Have Known and Loved," published in *Fatal Flaw* in 2020. She is editor and curator for the Voices on Addiction column at The Rumpus. Find her on Instagram at @kellyblog or Twitter at @stareenite.

Meredith Trede's collection, *Tenement Threnody,* is from Main Street Rag Press. SFA State University Press published *Field Theory.* A Toadlily Press founder, her chapbook, *Out of the Book,* was in *Desire Path.* Extensive journal publications include *Barrow Street, Cortland Review, Friends Journal, Gargoyle, Witness,* and *The Paris Review.* She was granted residencies at Blue Mountain Center, Ragdale, Saltonstall, and the Virginia Center for Creative Arts. She serves on the Slapering Hol Press Advisory Committee. www.meredithtrede.com.

Susan O'Dell Underwood directs the creative writing program at Carson-Newman University near Knoxville, Tennessee. Besides two chapbooks, she has one full-length collection, *The Book Of Awe* (Iris, 2018). Her poems and creative nonfiction appear and are forthcoming in all sorts of publications, including *Still: The Journal, Alaska Quarterly Review, Calyx,* and *Ecotone.* She is currently working on a chapbook of poems about her mother's dementia.

Beth Walker is a writing consultant whose work has recently appeared in *Tiferet*, *The Buddhist Poetry Review*, *Persephone's Daughters*, and *Hemingway Shorts*, among others. Her chapter on teaching #MeToo content appears in the scholarly collection *#MeToo and Literary Studies*, published by Bloomsbury, fall 2021.

Kristy Webster-Gonzalez is the author of *The Gift of an Imaginary Girl*. She,'s the recipient of an MFA in Creative Writing from Pacific Lutheran University and a Master's in Teaching from Heritage University. Her work has appeared in *Lunch Ticket*, *Pithead Chapel*, *Shark Reef Literary Magazine*, *The Molotov Cocktail*, *Connotation Press*, *Into the Void*, as well as the anthology *Two Countries*, published by Red Hen Press.

Kim Welliver lives in Utah with her husband and daughters. A Pushcart nominee, her work has been published in numerous journals and anthologies. When she is isn't writing, Kim works with special needs children.

Rochelle Williams lives in southern New Mexico. Her fiction and poetry have appeared in a number of publications, including *Desert Exposure, Earthships: A New Mecca Poetry Collection, The MacGuffin*, and *Menacing Hedge*. Her story "That Day" won first prize in the WOW Women on Writing 2020 Flash Fiction Contest. She holds an MFA in fiction from Vermont College of Fine Arts and is working on a novel about the French early modernist painter, Pierre Bonnard.

Genoa Yáñez-Alaniz is a mother of four, an educator, and a community organizer centering her work around advocacy for immigrants and refugees and language as resistance. Her poetry is published or forthcoming in *The Journal of Latina Critical Feminism, Cutthroat: Puro Chicanx Writers of the 21st Century, I Sing: The Body, Cloud Women's Quarterly Journal*, and *Rogue Agent*.

Meg Yardley lives in the San Francisco Bay Area. Her work has recently appeared or is forthcoming in publications including *Salamander, SWWIM, Bodega Magazine, Glass: A Journal of Poetry*, and the *Women's Review of Books*.

Jane Zwart teaches at Calvin University, where she also co-directs the Calvin Center for Faith & Writing. Her poems have been published in *Ploughshares, TriQuarterly*, and *Poetry*, as well as other journals and magazines.

About MER

MER - Mom Egg Review is a literary magazine that is focused on motherhood. We publish poetry, fiction, creative prose, and art, about all aspects of motherhood and the life experiences of women, by mothers and others, in an annual print issue and online. We believe that motherhood provides compelling and wide-ranging subject matter for literature. We believe in the importance of showcasing work that deals with diverse experiences of motherhood, and in supporting mother writers at all stages of their writing lives.

MER

MER - Mom Egg Review Back Issues Available:

Vol. 19	2021, Paper, 129 pp. $18
Vol. 18 "Home"	2020, Paper, 129 pp. $18
Vol. 17	2019, Paper, 117 pp. $18
Vol. 16 "Play and Work"	2018, Paper, 118 pp. $18
Vol. 15	2017 Paper, 123 pp. $18
Vol. 14 "Change"	2016 Paper, 128 pp. $18
Vol. 13 "Compassionate Action"	2015 Paper, 154 pp. $18
Vol. 12	2014 Paper, 150 pp. $18
Vol. 11 "Mother Tongue"	2013 Paper, 125 pp. $18
Vol. 10 "The Body"	2012 Paper, 120 pp. $18
Vol. 9	2011 Paper, 120 pp. $18
Vol. 8 "Lessons"	2010 Paper, 120 pp. $18
Vol. 7	2009 Paper, 124 pp. $18

*Plus US shipping $3.50 for the first book, $1.00 for each additional book.

Subscribe to *MER*
One year $18
Two years $36

Order at www.momeggreview.com (Click "Shop")
or mail your order with a check to:

Mom Egg Review
PO Box 9037
Bardonia, NY 10954

Contact: MERliterary@gmail.com

Email for info about discounts for quantity purchases and for classroom use, or for out-of-country shipping.

www.ingramcontent.com/pod-product-compliance
Lightning Source LLC
Chambersburg PA
CBHW081324020726
47506CB00005B/1173